World University Library

The World University Library is an international series
of books, each of which has been specially commissioned.
The authors are leading scientists and scholars from all over
the world who, in an age of increasing specialisation, see the
need for a broad, up-to-date presentation of their subject.
The aim is to provide authoritative introductory books for
students which will be of interest also to the general
reader. Publication of the series takes place in Britain,
France, Germany, Holland, Italy, Spain, Sweden
and the United States.

Frontispiece : Testing 'the fiveness of five'.

Philippe Muller

The Tasks
of Childhood

**translated from the French by
Anita Mason**

World University Library

**McGraw-Hill Book Company
New York Toronto**

© Philippe Muller 1969
Translation © George Weidenfeld and Nicolson Ltd
Library of Congress Catalog Card Number: 67–26358
Phototypeset by BAS Printers Limited, Wallop, Hampshire, England
Printed by Officine Grafiche Arnoldo Mondadori, Verona, Italy

Contents

Following usual practice, the child is 'he' throughout this book unless the context distinguishes boys from girls.

1 Childhood's changing status

Since the beginning of this century children have been growing up bigger and faster. They now learn more and they learn it in different ways. They grow up in a new type of family where discipline takes different forms. They have become a more important part of society. While they are still babies there are special clinics ready for them. When they are a little older they can be put in nursery schools, open to a younger and younger age group. As soon as they enter school they are surrounded with attention. They are coaxed through their elementary schooling, steered into the channels of secondary education and trained in laboratories and workshops, which are better and better equipped and cost more and more to keep up. Teenagers are becoming increasingly important as a group. Governments worry that they are not providing enough for a younger generation which beleaguers society like a foreign army and calls for more and more to be spent on it.

Are these changes for the good, or are they dangerous? Is childhood in the process of losing its identity, or is it simply coming to be recognised for what it is – the launching on life of a new generation which will itself shortly be responsible for the general good? These are questions which modern man cannot avoid. He may not any longer disregard the state of childhood. That he may not, is surely the most important aspect of modern childhood: it has become, as rarely before, the concern and preoccupation of adults.

Of course for hundreds of thousands of years men have been born, have matured into adulthood, have made new homes and in turn have brought up their own children before growing old and dying. Yet the status of childhood varies according to the type of society, and in our modern industrial societies it is changing rapidly.

Although all these changes are accelerated today, they began before our time. They accompanied the social upheaval which turned traditional society upside-down in a few generations and

1 Phases in Western demographic evolution : 1 : birth and death 'natural' and a stable or gradually increasing population in traditional society ; 2 : a marked drop in mortality, birth-rate steady, greatly increased population ; 3 : birth-rate also drops, the population increases less rapidly, giving an older average age ; 4 : birth-rate steadies or begins gradually to rise, the population starts to increase again but appears more balanced. In each phase childhood has a particular status.

created from it the diversified society of today.

At this point it is useful to distinguish four phases in man's recent history, each of which corresponds to a certain type of social equilibrium and involves a certain attitude to childhood (figure 1).

First phase

In this first phase, birth and death were 'natural'. Birth-control was not practised, but medicine was not very effective either. There was accordingly a high birth-rate and a high mortality. In this way the total population remained constant, with a very gradual increase which was often brutally interrupted by war, famine or epidemic. An investigation by Jean Fourastié and his pupils yielded the following biographical statistics for Normandy in the year 1730:

Very high infant mortality – one in four newborn children.
Short life-expectancy – less than twenty-five years.
Only 425 men per thousand attain marriageable age (average age twenty-seven) and only 440 women per thousand (average age twenty-five).
The average age at death of married people is fifty-one.
The average duration of a marriage is seventeen ('the eternal vows are sworn for fifteen years', says Fourastié . . .).
There are on average 4·1 births per marriage; the average child loses one of his parents by fourteen.
The man who reaches fifty has seen, on average, nine people die in his own family or immediate circle.

The consequences of such a demographic structure for the individual were harsh; he was fragile, easily replaceable, and so of little importance. He was only a link in the chain of generations, a cell in the all-encompassing social body which could replace him automatically without anyone noticing it.

This social structure had no tenderness for the child. He was tolerated provided he grew up as quickly as possible. Childhood

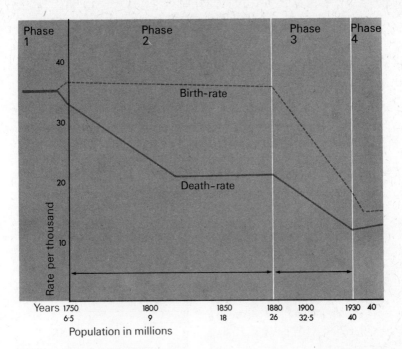

Phase 1   Phase 2   Phase 3   Phase 4

Rate per thousand

Birth-rate

Death-rate

| Years | 1750 | 1800 | 1850 | 1880 | 1900 | 1930 | 40 |
| | 6·5 | 9 | 18 | 26 | 32·5 | 40 | |

Population in millions

was considered a necessary evil. Authority was firmly exercised by the older generation, the guardians of tradition, who had no compunction about making the child conform to it.

In Western society, it must be added, the lot of the child seems to have been harsher than elsewhere. There are many primitive societies where the child is believed to be the reincarnation of an ancestor and thus to have a kind of personal guardian angel at his service, at least until the initiation ceremony. Naturally, it would be unthinkable to beat one's grandfather! But no such religious considerations soften the general severity of European traditions. Three influences have affected the status of childhood in Europe:

The Roman tradition, which lies behind the law and bestows all authority, even the power of life and death, on the father of the family.

The Germanic tradition, which survives in customs, and attaches importance to the group of 'peers' with whom the child gains experience of life – often in combat – and from which he only emerges at adolescence when he has

2 In traditional society the age-groups form a pyramid because there are fewer people alive with every year of age. There is a particularly high mortality in childhood, less than half the population reaching marriageable age.

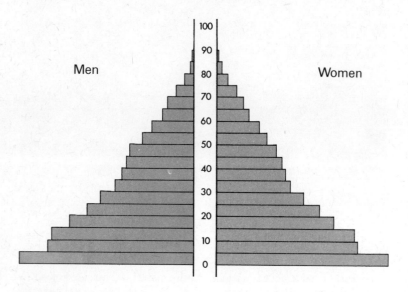

achieved his first feat of arms, or the masterpiece of his 'apprenticeship'.

The Christian tradition, which is a blend of the preceding two. This tradition is in fact ambiguous. According to the doctrine of original sin the child is born already tainted, and the severity of his upbringing must prevent the effects of this natural corruption. On the other hand, Jesus commands men to return to the state of childhood, which implies that it is the normal state and merits protection and respect. (The Church has been opening homes and institutions for children in various places for the past thousand years.)

In the Middle Ages childhood was short. This can be seen from children's clothes and also from the ages of famous lovers (Juliet's 'not fourteen', and Romeo not sixteen). The child often had to take the reins of life at a very early age, replacing the father who had died or the mother worn out by childbirth and illness. Society seems to have watched the destruction of childhood with almost

3 The child-adult.
Velasquez :
The Infanta
Margareta Theresia
(Kunsthistorisches
Museum, Vienna)

complete indifference. Little Cosette in Hugo's *Les Miserables*, and the orphans of the countryside, had the most horrifying fate. Corporal punishment was common and barbaric (all the more so for being common coin among adults as well). The death penalty was inflicted on children in the late eighteenth century; in France a case is recorded of a ten-year-old child who was hanged for the accidental killing of a friend.

Second phase

Round about 1750 the mortality rate fell in the West and the population figures rose dramatically. The causes of this first demographic revolution are uncertain. It seems that the invention of the microscope, which revealed the quantity of bacteria existing in

12

4 and **5** The Romantic view of
youth and childhood
(*left*) Weckerlin : Friedrich Schiller.
(Schiller National-Museum, Marbach)
(*right*) Madame Vigée-Lebrun and her
daughter ; self-portrait (Louvre, Paris)

ordinary drinking-water, gave rise to a considerable improvement
in everyday hygiene. In the West, this increase in population later
combined with rapid industrialisation and the expansion of towns.
However, at first the child's position was not much affected – if
anything it grew worse. The first legislation on labour in the textile
mills forbade the employment of children under five (they were
useful in the spinning-mills because, being so small, they could slip
under the machines to repair the broken threads). As late as 1866
the International Alliance of Workers praised

the trend in modern industry to enlist the co-operation of adolescents and
children of both sexes in the great movement of social production as *a
legitimate and logical step forward*, even though the weight of opinion in the
capital has made it appear something shocking. In a rational society, every
child *over the age of nine years* should be a productive worker. [My italics].

However, in certain circles the attitude to children was changing.
Since the eighteenth century the privileged classes had been reading
Rousseau and had assimilated his central affirmation that 'the child
has modes of feeling, thinking and existing which are proper to
him'. Gradually, the wish to speed up the child's maturation died
away. The desirable thing now was to keep the child in his state of
innocence, to protect him against the dangers of adult society,
against the pain and sterility of civic responsibility. Romanticism
made adolescence a privileged state. Even fashion emphasised the
freedom and spontaneity of youth. A new tenderness enveloped the
child ; fashionable ladies played for their own amusement *à la
Sévigné* (as Mme Vigée-Lebrun and her children).

Third phase

What had at first only characterised the well-to-do became general
after the so-called 'second demographic revolution'. After the

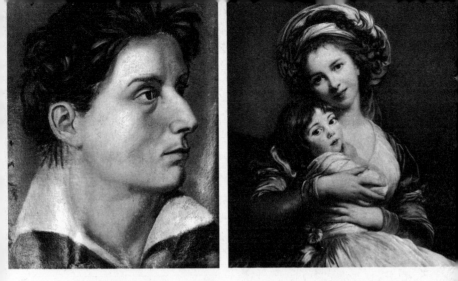

death-rate, the birth-rate dropped, so rapidly that the distribution of the age-groups now looked like the outline of an urn (figure 6). Throughout society, the proportion of children to adults decreased.

Here again the causes of the development are complex. We tend to imagine that a profound change of attitude took place; people with children knew that they had to provide for their education, and that they had to do so for a period which was becoming progressively longer with the introduction of compulsory education, the raising of the lower age-limit for work in the mills and the extension of professional training. However, to this must be added a factor of a more sociological nature. The typical family of the period now lived in the town not the country, and it played a more limited role. Previously it had played a number of economic roles. It had often been a productive unit in farming; and for a long time it remained the unit for providing services (such as food, clothing, repairs), and the centre of leisure activities. In the town it tended to restrict itself to the role of consumer. Household needs were provided mainly by the father, sometimes by both parents, but in general work was done away from home, and home was gradually reduced to the place where one slept, ate and spent what little time was left free in a life which was becoming more and more heavily burdened. Thirdly, the family was breaking up. The number of older people

6 With a declining birth-rate, the youngest age-groups no longer fill up the ranks of their predecessors. Hence the 'urn' shape assumed by the diagram.

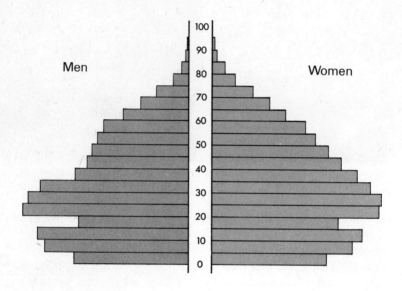

in the household diminished. In the country two generations had often lived under the same roof, and separate families had combined in working the land. In the town the adult circle shrank to the mother and father. On the other hand the number of children also diminished. Even in the previous stages of social evolution the average number of births had been comparatively low – 4·1 per marriage (see above). But it fell lower still and very large families, although still to be found in the country, became exceptional or non-existent in the towns.

All this had direct consequences for the child and his social position. A point not so far emphasised is that hitherto the child had had little contact with his parents. But now parents and children were left face to face, and the children were more dependent on them than ever, both for subsistence and for guidance. The child

7 The third historical phase sees the child behaving at all times as if under the eye of a severe and exacting father.

15

was no longer surrounded and protected by a little republic of other children who stood between him and his parents. Parental judgment – sometimes praise but usually punishment – touched him directly. He therefore began to think about and to anticipate his parents' probable reactions, which were responsible for his socialisation. In doing so he internalised the norms of behaviour which surrounded him. He began to behave, even when alone, as if under the eye of a severe and exacting father. From then onwards every child, like Aeneas, carried on his back this idealised ancestor who was to become his conscience.

From this it is clear that in future the child would be 'inner-directed', in Riesman's phrase. His position evolved. He became important both in the family and in society. He became more 'valuable': on the one hand he cost more to keep and to educate,

8 In the last phase of demographic evolution the child becomes the 'little prince' whose rights must be respected by society. In its Declaration of the Rights of the Child, the United Nations proclaimed ten principles which, if universally practised, would bring about the greatest social revolution of all time.

on the other hand his parents invested more love and also more ambition in him. In many cases they wished him to achieve things which had been denied to them. They considered that his success would bring them some sort of return from life. This feeling gave rise to an ambivalent attitude towards the child, ranging from extreme indulgence when he seemed to fulfil the hopes placed in him to extreme severity when he disappointed them, or looked as though he might. Education thus became a speedier process, as if the parents' generation were eager to see the child reach a better position than they had. It has recently been demonstrated that this attitude corresponds quite closely to that of the small contractor of the last century, who made great sacrifices for the sake of industrial and commercial success, risked everything, invested everything, and won success by sheer hard work. (This is the 'entrepreneurial' education of Miller and Swanson.)

Fourth phase

The third phase of demographic evolution, the phase we have just considered, brought the child to a social position he had never before held. He became the little prince around whom everything revolved. A glance at the Declaration of the Rights of the Child, of which the first (American) version emerged from national conferences on the problems of children and the last version was adopted and 'unanimously proclaimed' by the United Nations General Assembly on 20 November 1959, convinces one that if these principles were to be henceforward observed in every country a revolution would take place beside which all the revolutions of the past would fade into insignificance. For the rights stated are universal, 'without distinction or discrimination on account of race, colour, sex, language, religion, political or other status . . .' (Principle 1). They proclaim that

The child shall . . . be given opportunities to enable him to develop physically, mentally, morally, spiritually and socially . . . in conditions of freedom and dignity. (Principle 2)

The child shall enjoy the benefits of social security . . . . The child shall have the right to adequate nutrition, housing, recreation and medical services. (Principle 4)

The child is entitled to receive education, which shall be free and compulsory, at least in the elementary stages. (Principle 7)

The child shall not be admitted to employment before an appropriate minimum age; he shall in no case be caused or permitted to engage in any occupation or employment which would prejudice his health or education, or interfere with his physical, mental or moral development. (Principle 9)

He shall be brought up in a spirit of understanding, tolerance, friendship among peoples, peace and universal brotherhood and in full consciousness that his energy and talents should be devoted to the service of his fellow men. (Principle 10)

This preferential treatment of the child brings its problems, however. In the third phase the child began to depend too much on adults. In certain cultures, particularly the American, this strict dependence has above all tied the child to his mother, who is his first teacher and is often the head of the house while the father is out at work. During the wartime general conscription of 1942 the recruiting officers were obliged to exempt a large number of young people – one-fifth – purely on neuropsychiatric grounds. One of the psychiatrists involved in the examinations attributed the frequency of these personality disturbances to the fact that 'their parents, particularly their mothers, did too much for them, and for too long' (Strecker).

Society has changed with time. The social structures of the last century characterised by the small businessman, with an emphasis on individual initiative, have been succeeded by bigger and bigger enterprises forming complex social worlds, enveloping the individual in a tight, continuous network of obligations and anxieties. In these modern 'bureaucracies' the parental attitude changes. It is no longer as pushing as it was at the beginning of the century or as it still is in socially ambitious circles. It is child-centred in a completely different way. It combines care and understanding and also respect for what is right for the child. This democratic attitude relaxes the inner pressure created by too strict a conscience. It allows a certain flexibility. Increasingly the norm of behaviour is regulated not by the 'inner eye', but by a broad general consensus – the opinion of one's friends, the general feeling. The individual now tends to be 'other-directed' (Riesman). This new philosophy of education is without doubt related to the character of the more advanced societies – a flexible equilibrium between the age-groups which are now distributed in the form of a column (figure 9). Parents and teachers must therefore be helped to find the turning which leads from a rigid, moralistic type of education to a flexible one oriented towards the fulfilment of the individual. This is the task of the new child psychology.

9 In the fourth phase a greater balance is attained
between the age-groups, so that the total population
may now form something like a column, crowned
by a pyramid showing the very old. This is a development
towards a stable demographic structure.

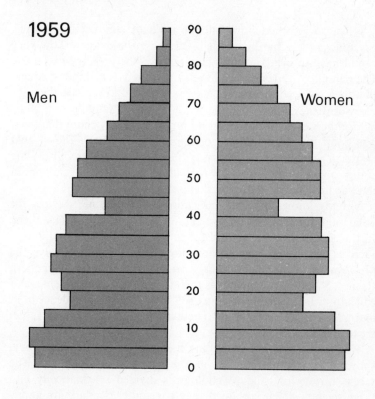

1959

Men

Women

When society laid down all the rules of conduct in advance, psychology was hardly needed. Young people knew how they would have to bring up their children even before they had them. The parents of today do not have this security. The kind of education they received themselves may have served to prepare them for the world they knew, but the world is now changing so rapidly before their eyes that they can no longer seriously claim that what was good for them will be good for their children. They would reproach themselves for preparing their children for an out-of-date reality much as they would for deciding to dress their children in the way they had been dressed themselves.

Nobody knows the ideal educational programme. Recipes for education may fail but on one can, in consequence, replace them. In this situation there is no resort to the 'guardians of tradition' – such as the clergy – or to any dogmas which would solve the problem. No experiments can be trusted except those of modern science. Scientific psychology is therefore called in to take charge of education. Is it capable of doing so? Can we have confidence in it, and what can we expect of it? These are the questions which I shall try to answer.

This book begins by describing the development of psychology, showing how it has reached its present view of childhood. The recent history of child psychology is divided schematically into three phases, which, although they constantly overlap, are nevertheless useful to differentiate, since they allow a clearer view of the solid achievements which have been made along the way.

1 First of all, as always in Western society, attention was focused on our access to reality. The question was how knowledge came about, or in other words what intelligence – in its quantitative aspect ('intellectual level') and its qualitative aspect ('the structure of intelligence') – consisted of.

2 However, the levels or modes of the adaptation do not explain

the reason for the action. At the beginning of the century the evolution and interplay of the child's basic drives became a question for research, and psychoanalysis, with its scope and limitations, began to gain ground.

3 Intelligence and motivation are two essential aspects of childhood. But they are often two incompatibles. It is necessary to go beyond the point where they conflict and see the child in concrete situations. The third phase of child psychology reconciles the previous points of view, combining them into an overall or 'global' view which is certainly much more complex but is also better adapted to the complexity of the thing itself – the innumerable faces of childhood.

2 Measuring intelligence

Every language has a word for a wise man and a word for a fool. Western languages, from Latin onwards, have been very well supplied in this respect. It is one area where, however rigid they may otherwise have become through writing, they still remain creative and are constantly being enriched with new terms.

People plainly differ in their capacity to adapt to new situations, whether human or impersonal. From this it is only a short step to the idea that a sort of quantitative ability exists to a greater or lesser degree in everyone. Earlier societies tended to mask these individual differences, except in the extreme cases of outstanding ability or of idiocy. The normal situations of life were simple and everyone, or nearly everyone, had the necessary mental resources to deal with them. In any case there was little room for exceptional talents. There was not enough variety in work for the idea of selection or professional vocation to make any practical sense. High posts in society were usually awarded for reasons other than competence, such as birth or the social position already held.

When the expansion of society introduced greater variety, the differences between people became more important. As social tasks grew more complicated, it became more obvious that certain people succeeded in them while others failed. The factors which contributed most to this realisation were the growth of towns and the education of children.

In the country even the idiot had a useful social role. He found some tasks which he was able to do – harvesting the crops, minding the animals – and he assumed the role of the scapegoat, the butt, the 'negative model'; he was pointed out to children as a lesson, to make them more obedient. But in the town he quickly lost his footing. When he could no longer perform socially respected tasks he was universally rejected and finally he was locked up. Moreover, compulsory education revealed the existence of children who had to struggle hard to grasp the rudiments of reading, writing and arithmetic, sometimes not even succeeding in the end. Until that time, instruction had been given only to those who showed an interest in it or were obviously capable of benefiting from it. The democratic ideal, which had been closely bound up with industrial society from the beginning, demanded that each person should be able to participate in public affairs and thus be able to read and write. In addition industrial work tended to call for higher and more varied aptitudes than traditional agricultural work. All these are reasons why elementary schooling became general in the last century, but its very universality disclosed problems of aptitude which had never been clearly seen before.

When they were recognised, they became associated with other problems of mental anomaly or abnormality. Little distinction was made between mental deficiency and mental degeneration occurring as part of a disease, until Esquirol's book on mental disorders in 1838. This provided the first distinction between idiocy (the term still covered all the degrees of mental deficiency) and mental disorder. The idiots, so to speak, were those who had always been mentally underprivileged and poor; the others were 'the poor who had once been rich'. The latter sometimes regained what they had lost, while it was unheard of, said Esquirol, for an idiot ever to achieve a higher level than his established one.

Esquirol distinguished degrees of idiocy according to the ability to use language. At the highest level of deficiency, language was still easy (German psychiatrists were later to describe a particular type of idiocy as *Salonblödsinn*, 'the idiocy of the drawing-room'). At the level below, language was difficult and vocabulary restricted. True idiocy began with those who could only manage isolated words or very short phrases; this led to a second stage where only syllables and cries were heard, and in the third and last stage there was no language, phrases, words or syllables.

We have mentioned that idiocy was at first thought irreversible,

10 Jean Étienne Esquirol
(1772–1840).

and the idiot ineducable. This harmonised well with the determinist ideas of the time, and was partly dictated by the need to describe the various forms of mental abnormality in very precise terms, such as would be used to describe particular species of animals. However, one famous 'natural experiment' at about the same time cast some doubt on the ineducability of mental defectives. Towards the end of the eighteenth century, a naked boy of about twelve was discovered in the forests of Aveyron. He was incapable of speech, ran on all fours, lay on his stomach to lap water, and fought with nails and teeth if attacked. Pinel pronounced him an idiot. Itard did not accept this judgment. He attributed the child's deficiencies to the isolation in which he had lived and undertook to educate him. But he had little success and abandoned the attempt before he had brought his 'savage' to a socially acceptable condition. One man, however, had been more impressed by the progress made than by the apparent failure. This was another psychiatrist, Eduard Seguin, a pupil of both Itard and Esquirol. In 1837 Seguin opened a school for mental defectives and quickly attracted attention both by his method and by his success. His example was soon followed by

Guggenbuhl in Switzerland and White in England, and in 1846 an American commission in Massachusetts began to study the question of special schooling for mental defectives. In 1870 there were no less than eighty private and public schools for deficient children and adults in America, Europe and Australia. At the end of the century there was scarcely an educational system of any importance that did not have its 'special classes'.

In 1904 the French Minister of Education set up a commission to coordinate and systematise education for the deficient, and called on the help of Alfred Binet. It soon became obvious that one of the first necessities was an objective criterion of what constituted deficiency and required special educational measures. It was not possible to rely on the judgment of the school-teacher, who frequently confused cases of retardation with cases of simple disturbance or lack of emotional adaptation.

Binet and his colleague Simon were acquainted with the earlier work on 'intelligence'. They knew that nothing useful was gained by working from the previous theoretical conceptions, for instance in defining intelligence by speed of reaction or by memory. Instead they adopted a completely different type of yardstick. They wanted to measure global ability to solve minor problems, such as those encountered in everyday life, not to measure hypothetical faculties. They also had to find a manageable test, easily administered and not too long. The essential thing however was to arrange the tasks according to the average age at which they could be performed rather than according to their particular characteristics.

Three successive scales (1905, 1908 and 1911) resulted from these efforts. They defined precisely the idea of *mental age*, which had already been suggested from time to time, but which after the success of Binet–Simon scale was bound to have considerable influence. It was an *operative concept*, related directly to the scale which was constructed for its evaluation, which indicated the child's place in normal mental development. (If he was developing at the same average rate as all his contemporaries, he would have a mental age corresponding to his real age; if he was retarded, his mental age would be inferior, and it would be superior if he were particularly brilliant, that is to say capable of solving problems which could ordinarily only be solved by older people.) Mental age therefore implies a comparison with the real or chronological age. This correspondence was not in fact clarified by Binet himself, who died just when his work was taking its final shape, but by one of the pioneering German psychologists, W. Stern (1912). In its final form it became the *intelligence quotient*, or *IQ*, of which wide practical use is still made.

The scale and its use

In 1908 the American, Henry Goddard, adapted the Binet–Simon scale for Anglo-Saxon use, and wide experimentation with it in the United States quickly superseded the European applications of the scale. Thus before the First World War, the initiative had passed to the Anglo-Saxon psychologists, who quickly realised the necessity of tidying up the imperfect instrument they had borrowed. The work was done by L. M. Terman of Stanford University (hence the name of the revised scale – *the Stanford revision*) who remodelled it almost completely. He gave precise and rigorous instructions about the use of the scale, as regards both evaluation and the grading of responses. He also systematised the procedure, providing six tests for each age group, and standardised it carefully, taking pains to ensure that he had a representative population, that is, a sample of subjects about whom generalisations could be made. In short, he transformed a brilliant but incomplete draft into a trustworthy and robust instrument.

In the form it assumed from then on, the Binet–Simon intelligence scale contained six tests for each age group from three to ten, eight tests for twelve and another six again for fourteen, sixteen and eighteen years. The tests cover widely varying fields. At five, for instance, the child has to:

compare two weights
name four colours
compare three pairs of faces and choose the 'prettiest'
define at least four ideas out of six
do two puzzles out of three satisfactorily in one minute
perform three tasks

The scoring is done in months. The child is first of all given the age in months at which he passes all the tests. A number of months is then added corresponding to the isolated tests for higher age groups which he can also do. The following score would therefore be given for a child of five years three months (63 months) who performed the following tests.

all the tests for 5 years	60
all the tests for 6 years	12
5 tests for 7 years (2 months each)	10
2 tests for 8 years	4
1 test for 9 years	2
3 tests for 10 years	6
0 tests for 12 years	0

94 months

This example illustrates the actual method. One begins at the age at which one thinks the child will be able to do all the tests. (Preliminary tests can be carried out to give a quick estimate of the probable level, so as to avoid exposing the child to a series of failures.) One then continues up through the age groups until

11 The IQ is 'normally distributed' : most of
the population are close to the mean (100), and
fewer cases are found the further one goes from
this central point. Two-thirds of the population
fall between 85 and 115 (the 'norm'), one-
sixth above 115, and one-sixth below 85.

the child fails every test. One is then left with a score in months
which can be compared with the chronological age in months to
give the intelligence quotient: $IQ = \dfrac{94}{63} \times 100 = 149$. (The US
version, also used in Britain, no longer derives IQs this way, but
simply obtains scores of a child relative to those of his age group.)

Distribution of IQs

By definition the average IQ is 100; IQs above 100 indicate a good
or superior intellectual level, and IQs below 100 indicate various
degrees of retardation or deficiency. However we need a further
piece of information in order to understand the score. We need to
know the distribution of IQs around the mean of 100. Is it a normal
distribution – that is to say, does it conform, with allowance for
standard errors, to the theoretical error curve (Gauss) or the bell-
shaped curve? What is the value of the standard deviation, or
index of dispersal of the scores?

Terman's work supplied answers to these two questions. The IQ
has a normal distribution, like most measures used in biology
(height, weight, grasp) and psychology (figure 11). The standard
deviation, which varies slightly with age, is in the region of 15.
Other psychologists when constructing tests have kept this value in
converting their scores to the equivalent IQ (particularly in the case
of Weschler's scale, known under its American title of WISC,
which is now becoming very popular). It is thus possible to place
any subject quickly in reference to the rest of the population, once it
is established that two-thirds of the population fall between one
standard deviation below and one standard deviation above the
mean ($-\sigma$ and $+\sigma$). The child used as an illustration above comes
more than three standard deviations above the mean, a performance
equalled or surpassed by only two people in a thousand (table 1).

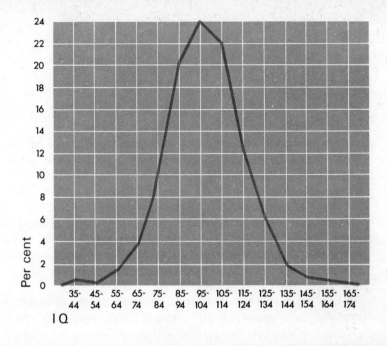

Table 1 Significance of IQ scores

An IQ of	is equalled or surpassed by
160	1 person in 10,000
140	7 persons in 1,000
130	3 persons in 100
120	11 persons in 100
110	27 persons in 100
100	50 persons in 100
90	73 persons in 100
80	89 persons in 100
70	97 persons in 100

The predictive value of IQ

It must be emphasised that the intelligence quotient does not measure a faculty or a specific function. Through the construction of the scales used to measure it, it indicates the probability of an individual correctly performing tasks of increasing difficulty. The IQ may thus be interpreted as a 'social level of functioning', which emphasises the way this measure is rooted in a diversified industrial society. We prefer to define the various levels of IQ by the social standards to which they correspond rather than by the traditional terminology of intelligence. For this purpose it is useful to refer to a composite table (see opposite).

In Europe, people with a superior IQ have a chance of studying successfully at a university. 105 seems to be the lowest IQ which guarantees a secondary education without difficulty; between 85 and 95 the child manages to follow the normal educational course, but with one or two failures along the way; 75 seems to be the required IQ for instruction in a special class; the retarded (50–70) only learn to read with tremendous effort and make scarcely any progress; and below 50 (imbeciles 25–50) there is no point in thinking in terms of progress, although simple occupational tasks can be done; idiots (below 25) learn virtually nothing and are cases for institutions.

In the academic field, according to the classic English work of Burt, the correspondence between IQ and literary and scientific subjects (from 0·45 to 0·60) is higher than between IQ and handwriting (0·21), manual work (0·18) and drawing (0·15). This is shown in psychology by a correlation index which ranges from $+1·00$ – perfect positive correspondence – to $-1·00$ – perfect negative correspondence – through 0·00, which indicates no relationship at all between the items compared. There is nothing mysterious in these figures. They simply indicate that if children are

Table 2 Social levels corresponding to various levels of IQ

130 mean IQ of people obtaining a university degree

120 mean IQ of those who pass their *baccalauréat* (school-leaving certificate giving access to university)

115 mean IQ of first-year students at a typical four-year 'college' (USA type)
mean IQ of children of professional people

110 mean IQ of children leaving secondary school (high school, USA)
50–50 chance of staying successfully to the end of a college course

105 50–50 chance of success in a secondary school with a long course of education

100 mean IQ of total population

90 mean IQ of children from poor urban homes or from rural districts
the adult can perform tasks requiring some judgment, e.g. using a sewing machine or working on an assembly line

75 50–50 chance of going to secondary school (high school, USA)
the adult can manage a small trade, hold a place in an orchestra

60 the adult can repair furniture, grow vegetables, be an electrician's mate

50 the adult can do simple carpentry and domestic jobs

40 the adult can cut the lawn, do the washing.

grouped by IQ the results will be more homogeneous in composition and geometry than in drawing, and if they are grouped by their drawing ability, the groups will be very heterogeneous with regard to grammar or arithmetic.

Because of the usefulness of the IQ in predicting the educational ability of a child, and later in directing the adolescent towards a professional training or placing the adult in a specific job, it is obviously essential to determine the stability of the individual's IQ. The IQ cannot in fact be used as an instrument of social classification unless two successive measurements of it correspond, allowing for errors. Research on this aspect has somewhat tempered the initial optimism and enthusiasm.

The deceptions which have come to light in practice have obliged psychologists to refine their methods and to introduce more and more complex statistical techniques in order to define more accurately the errors of measurement and the degree of confidence which can be placed in an isolated measurement. The most important progress has resulted from the repetition of estimates of intellectual level in what are called *longitudinal* studies – studies on the same subjects, who are retested at different times in their development. One of these studies is particularly rich in suggestions about the evolution of the IQ: this is the study directed by Nancy Bayley at the University of California, Berkeley, in which the subjects were followed up from their first year until they reached maturity.

It has obviously not been possible to cover the complete span of age groups – over eighteen years – with the Binet–Simon scale alone, even in the various forms worked out by Terman. Special instruments have to be used during the period before language has developed; these have been worked out at the University of California for the first year of life and for the period of infancy up to school age. After adolescence there is a choice between the Binet–Simon test in one of its forms and the Weschler scale for adults. In this way it is possible to compare the same subjects by different means, in age groups spread out through the whole period of development (in all at 38 successive stages).

One conclusion is immediately apparent: the intellectual level is composed of types of behaviour which differ so much according to age that it is impossible to predict the intelligence of a very young child. The first year of life and the period before mastery of language is attained never give grounds for a valid prognosis. (In technical terms the correlation between the pre-language measurements and later measurements is of the order of 0·00.) The most precocious child in this age group may not even reach the mean at seventeen years (figure 12). What we speak of as intelligence is therefore made up of various aptitudes which develop unevenly in each individual, and a child's sensori-motor skill at an early age does not in any way forecast his academic skill in later life.

Secondly, the variability of scores changes from age group to age group and, in addition, individuals themselves are of varying stability (in the sense that some of their scores vary more than others). No relationship can be discerned between these variations and the intelligence level (although more significant relationships do exist between intelligence and the child's environment).

However, one must be careful not to throw out the baby with the bathwater. Although certain individuals show spectacular changes of position relative to the mean, on the whole forecasts become increasingly reliable as the child grows older or as two measurements become more closely approximated. This can be seen from figure 13, which shows that the later the measurements the higher the correlation between two successive measurements. (A correlation higher than 0·80, as is found in the measurement after seven, permits a reasonable forecast within the limits of practical certainty, but even so there will always be one child in six whose classification alters when the measurement is repeated.)

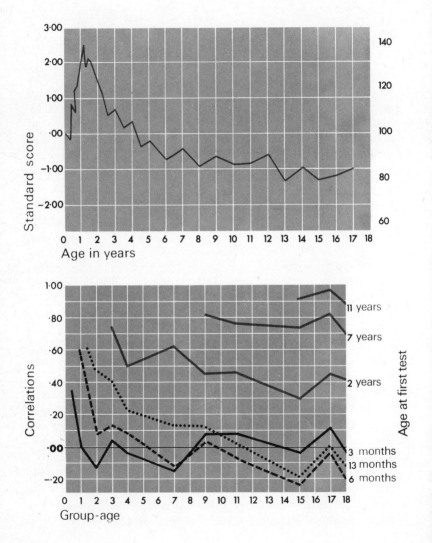

12 (*top*) Longitudinal studies, which follow the same child or group of children throughout their development, show that the IQ is not absolutely constant. Here Case F.14 is followed through in the Berkeley Growth Study ; she has a very superior score at the beginning, but is only at the mean when a little over four years old, and is at the lower limit of the norm at seventeen years. In other words, the IQ does not have any absolute value ; it indicates a person's approximate ranking in a group of contemporaries.

13 (*bottom*) Correlations between successive intelligence tests have been calculated in a group followed up from one to eighteen years (the curves show series of tests). The correlations between the measurements obtained before the second year and those obtained later are in the region of zero (indicating that there is no relationship between the measurements compared). After two years, however, the correlations reach a significant level, which becomes still higher after the first ten years. In other words, the later the measurement, the greater its significance, in spite of individual cases (such as that of F.14) which may show vagaries of development.

Refining measurements by analysing aspects of intelligence

Longitudinal studies emphasise the diversity of the behaviour patterns which are included in the general term 'intelligence', and which enable the individual to adapt to the demands of industrial society. In another field, the progress made in statistical analysis has permitted the analysis of 'intellectual' performance. This was at first a rather hesitant process because of the complex calculations involved, but since the war it has gained increasing momentum owing to the sophisticated calculating machines which have been available for research work.

A detailed account of these calculations is beyond the scope of this book, but in principle they are not difficult to understand. From a number of separate performances, each measured by a suitable test, a score for each individual is obtained. From this a table of figures (called a 'matrix') is produced, in which the columns usually represent the tests (performances), and the horizontal lines represent the individuals who have done them. Correlations between the columns are calculated. In this way a second matrix, comprising the correlation coefficients, is obtained, in which the lines and columns now show the tests which are being studied. The object of factor analysis is to fix the number of 'dimensions' which in combination produce the empirical coefficients one started with.

In 1904 the Englishman Spearman had remarked that intellectual tests generally maintained a positive correlation, although less than unity (perfect correlation). He therefore decided that the same single dimension entered into all these items (explaining the correlation), although each one also carried its own specific factor (explaining why the correlation was less than perfect). In his view, therefore, intelligence must be the product of the inter-play of two factors (the bi-factorial theory of intelligence) – one general (which he simply called g to emphasise its abstract and operational nature) and the other specific.

The verification of this hypothesis took many years and it was not until 1927 that Spearman published his results. The picture had become rather more complicated in the process. Within the realm of intelligence, which was now clearly distinguished from memory (another 'factor') and personality (still more factors), Spearman had been obliged at Burt's insistence to recognise performance groupings which referred to factors which were still common to a number of tests but were less universal than the g factor. (These were the *group factors*, of which the main ones from that time were the 'verbal factor' v, the 'numerical factor' n, and the 'spatial factor' s.) This led to a hierarchic theory of intelligence (figure 14, top) which rather resembled the hierarchy of a traditional society, with its king, aristocracy and people.

14 (*top*) Spearman's analysis of intelligence (1927) led to an hierarchic theory of intelligence. At the top was a general factor (g), which was present in every performance carried out by the subject; on the next level were the group factors (v) (verbal), (n) (numerical), etc., characteristic of particular types of performance, and finally the specific factors, s_1, s_2, etc., which affected particular performances (such as, in the verbal group, the solving of anagrams). (*centre*) Thurston's work resulted in the isolation of a certain number of primary factors of equal importance — V, N, P etc. Each measurement was still affected by a specific factor — s_1, s_2, etc. (*bottom*) Meili's conception of intelligence postulates a number of general factors, resembling mental functions, which automatically participate in every mental act; each act involves perception, memory and reasoning. This gives us an analysis of intelligence which meets the requirements of the mental structure, instead of relying on abstract factors which are too much determined by the tests employed.

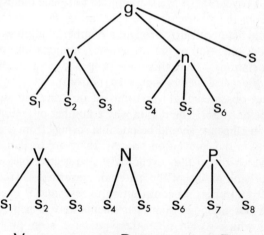

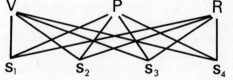

The American Thurstone soon countered with a more democratic and egalitarian model. By generalising Spearman's methods of calculation and bringing the resources of algebra and multi-dimensional geometry to bear on the problem, he conducted his analyses in such a way as to isolate independent *primary factors*, the sum of which would constitute traditional 'intelligence' (figure 14, centre). In this scheme the group factors appear again but in capitals, while the general factor has disappeared.

Many other models were proposed. Some psychologists argued for a large number of specific factors linked to each type of performance, and loosely and rather artificially grouped into more collective factors (one might call this the anarchic theory of intelligence). The Swiss psychologist Meili attempted to rescue the psychological reality from the abstractions of calculation. He observed that the intellectual act necessarily brought a number of abilities into play – perception, retention of past experience, imagination (or power of free association) – and therefore proposed a model featuring a *number of general factors* (figure 14, bottom).

Bossuet observed that variations of doctrine are sure signs of ignorance or doubt. The reason why a number of factorial conceptions of intelligence should be possible springs from a certain lack of rigidity in the calculation process: there are certain elements of choice which reveal the psychologist's subjective bias rather than the underlying nature of the material. Nevertheless factor analysis has made an important contribution to research. It has enabled us to refine our methods of measurements and to achieve a degree of detail which would not otherwise have been easily attained. Above all it helps in the construction of composite tools for measuring intelligence, and is the psychologist's guarantee that he knows as much as possible about his subject, whether for the purposes of research or practical application. (See figure 15.)

15 One of the most important practical applications of factor analysis is the general aptitude battery drawn up by the USES. This measures ten factors recognised as playing a decisive role in professional life. The diagram shows the factorial composition of this battery.

Aptitude Factor	Test	Factor Loading	Multiple Factor Loading
G Intelligence	H Three dimensional space	0·450	0·602
	I Arithmetic reason	0·552	
	J Vocabulary	0·513	
V Verbal Aptitude	J Vocabulary	0·533	0·533
N Numerical Aptitude	D Computation	0·483	0·500
	I Arithmetic reason	0·438	
S Spatial Aptitude	F Two dimensional space	0·397	0·503
	H Three dimensional space	0·500	
P Form Perception	A Tool matching	0·520	0·549
	L Form matching	0·435	
Q Clerical Perception	B Name comparison	0·627	0·627
A Aiming	C H Markings	0·473	0·506
	K Mark making	0·423	
T Motor Speed	G Speed	0·709	0·780
	K Mark making	0·708	
F Finger Dexterity	O Assemble	0·595	0·629
	P Disassemble	0·486	
M Manual Dexterity	M Place	0·628	0·662
	N Turn	0·500	

Differential maturation according to the factors

The results of factor analysis make it possible to consider the evolution of global intelligence (or the intellectual level) in a new way. We already know that this term covers different types of behaviour; we may now be a little more precise.

Taking up the data from the Berkeley longitudinal study, P. R. Hofstaetter showed that they could be interpreted in terms of three factors which were to some extent parallel but whose relative role varied considerably with age (figure 16). At the earliest stage (about two months) until the start of the second year, the first factor, which he called *'sensori-motor alertness'*, was predominant. The second factor first appeared with negative loadings, rose to a peak at about the end of the second year, and then gradually faded out. Hofstaetter saw in this stage signs of a certain *persistence*, expressed in the child by the negativism of the 'grumpy' age. It was only the third factor, which gained predominance in the fourth year, that corresponded to what we understand by *'intelligence'*.

If the factorial composition of intelligence changes so completely between the first months of life and school age, it is clear that one cannot predict adult performance from the performance of a baby. However, these first results of Hofstaetter are still too crude. For the pre-school age as many as seven different factorial dimensions have been suggested, each one with a different evolution according to the individual. As soon as factorialised batteries of tests can be used, the very first measurements show all the diversity of adults.

In this respect there has been a shift of opinion. At one time it was believed, on the strength of the early English work of Spearman's school, that the *g* factor began by being predominant and that with the effect of age it became differentiated into various aptitudes – conforming, in this respect, to other organic developments. This opinion is still circulated as if it were a recognised

16 Factor analysis of the results of a longitudinal study reveals the diverging development of three principal factors relating to intelligence. The first (shown by a broken line) is dominant in the early months of life, but then fades out. The second (dotted line) plays an important role from the second to the fifth year and then also gradually disappears. The third (red line) gains importance at the age of about six and a half years and maintains a very high level from then on. It is only this third factor which really corresponds to what we mean by intelligence. The first on the whole reflects sensori-motor capacity, and the second an innate attitude – the negativism and grumpiness of the small child.

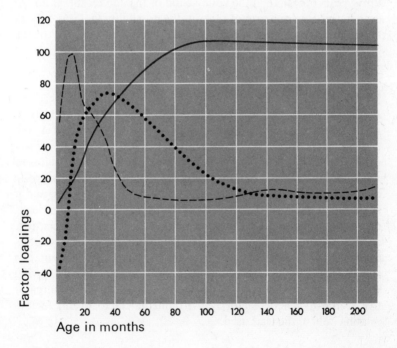

datum of psychology. In point of fact, subsequent testing has in no way confirmed this quasi-organic view of intellectual development. Since more carefully controlled groups have been used on which to establish the scores, we have progressed to less organic conceptions and have been forced to recognise that, although the factorial composition alters with age, it does so in an untidy way and not in the manner of a growing differentiation. On the contrary, a greater degree of integration has been found in adults (over thirty years old) than in the young child or the adolescent, although even in this case one cannot rule out the possibility that it is only an apparent phenomenon caused by the relative heterogeneity of the groups compared age for age.

Intelligence, heredity and environment

It is an obvious step to try to relate scores on intelligence tests to various circumstances which distinguish people. Everything relating to the measurement of intelligence comes into the realm of *differential psychology*, which is also concerned with whatever relates to racial or individual heredity, sex, and environment. Inter-group conflicts and tensions have sharply increased in recent years, and it is inevitable that the participants should have tried to pull science on to their side and thus support their prejudices. The scientists, on the other hand, caught between two fires, have made strenuous efforts towards objectivity. From the body of research on this subject I shall pick out three series of determinants (following P. E. Vernon, who has recently carried out one of the fullest comparative studies): genetic factors, environmental factors, and factors relating only to the tests used.

Genetic factors The most obvious genetic factor is race. It is notorious that children of different races – as in the USA, where this is an urgent problem – obtain significantly different scores, and after the First World War the superiority of white over black races was thought to be in this way scientifically proven. However, no account was taken at this time of difference in socio-economic status. When only strictly comparable groups are compared the difference almost vanishes, and what remains of it is too tenuous to be taken into practical consideration. (This is largely because the difference only appears between the means of each group and the distributions are almost exactly similar, so that in each group there are individuals who come above or below the mean of the other group.) In practice the majority of American psychologists and sociologists consider that the inter-group differences on intelligence tests are 'directly attributable to such environmental differences as educational opportunity and class position' (Berelson and Steiner 1964, p. 498).

The second major difference due to heredity is sex. However, this is never a pure difference either, in the sense that boys and girls are subjected from their earliest days to different educational pressures, and as they grow up must conform to social expectations and learn roles which cannot later be modified (see chapter 9). It is generally agreed that boys and men are better at mathematics, reasoning, manipulation of spatial relationships and mechanical tasks, while girls and women have better vocabulary, variety of expression and immediate memory.

There still remains an element of individual heredity. There have been heated discussions in this field of research, with opinions veering from one extreme to the other according to time and national origin. In the early years a great impression was made by the famous case of the Kallilak family publicised by Goddard (1912, 1914). Struck by the fact that a young defective girl had the same name as a prominent figure in public life, Goddard traced back the family tree of everyone with the same name and arrived at

17 Recent studies show significant differences between children from different socio-economic backgrounds. However, there are conflicting opinions as to what determines these differences; psychology now tends to favour a flexible explanation which takes a number of causative factors into account.

a young soldier at the time of the American Revolution who had fathered a child on a defective woman in an inn, and later contracted an honourable marriage and sired the second – respectable – branch of the family. The two parallel branches comprised, on one side, 480 descendants of whom 143 were known to have been defective and 46 to have been normal, and on the other side 496 descendants none of whom was recorded as being defective, delinquent, or illegitimate. It seemed obvious that heredity was largely responsible for these different destinies. Today we are more cautious, and observe that there cannot fail to be an important difference in environment between the child of a tavern girl, brought up in inevitably difficult conditions, and the son of a good family for whom everything is made easy. Goddard's demonstration made a particularly forceful impression in America since it flatly contradicted the prevailing belief that man was the child of circumstance, was born with the same opportunities as everyone else and was solely responsible for his destiny. In criticising Goddard there was a tendency to go to the other extreme and deny any influence at all to heredity – while European experts placed too much emphasis on it. It is now generally agreed that hereditary differences may account for divergences between people from the same environment, while differences of environment are the most important factor when people from varying social or cultural backgrounds are being compared.

Environmental factors There continue to be clear differences between children from different socio-economic backgrounds (figure 17). But although these differences are incontrovertible, they are too gross to shed light on exactly what in each environment favours or hinders intellectual growth. There is in fact a trend (which we shall see again in the analysis of the concrete situations the child is confronted with) to go beyond global verification. Thus

Father's occupational classification

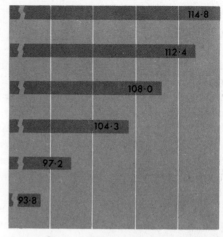

Professional — 114·8

Semi-professional & managerial — 112·4

Clerical, skilled trades, & retail business — 108·0

Semi-skilled, minor clerical, minor businesses — 104·3

Slightly skilled — 97·2

Day labourers, urban & rural — 93·8

95   100   105   110   115
Mean I Q s on revised Stanford-Binet

Vernon lists the following determining factors, each of which he sees as responsible for a differentiation in intelligence:

nutrition	teaching
perceptual deprivation	the language heard
restricted environment	the grammatical forms usual in the
family insecurity	environment
maternal domination	adolescent aspirations

Examples of the most influential determining factors will be reserved for chapter 5. A few words remain to be said here about factors relating to the tests used.

Factors relating to the tests themselves Each test has its own specific factor in the sense that some people, without being any more intelligent in general, will solve certain problems better than other people, even within the same field (the verbal, for example). However, it is necessary to go further than this and observe that it is impossible to construct tests which will be absolutely independent of the surrounding culture – the sub-culture of social class or environment, or the global culture in its historical context. It was originally thought that the measurement of intelligence touched on an aptitude which was innate, or at any rate free from any practical influence. Since then we have had to climb down; the expert knows today that his instruments impose a systematic distortion on his observations which he is forced to take into account. Klineberg tells a revealing story in this connection. He was using one of the forms of the Binet–Simon test, adapted for American use, in a mountainous part of Kentucky, and he asked his subject, a bright little boy of about ten: 'If you went to the store and bought six cents' worth of candy and gave the clerk ten cents, what change would you receive?' The boy replied, 'I never had ten cents, and if I had I wouldn't spend it for candy, and anyway candy is what your mother makes'. The examiner tried again: 'If you had taken ten cows to pasture for your father and six of them strayed, how many would you have left to drive home?' Like lightning came the reply: 'We don't have ten cows, but if we did and I lost six, I wouldn't dare go home.' The examiner tried a last time: 'If there were ten children in a school and six of them were out with measles, how many would there be in school?' 'None, because the rest would be afraid of catching it too.' One cannot conclude from this that the child is unable to subtract six from ten, only that he cannot manage to react to an imaginary situation and – even less – to one which is unreal to him. These attitudes implicit in the test situation call for the greatest caution when one is trying to compare groups. In a very general way intelligence scales are subtly impregnated with middle-class values, and people who do not share these values from the outset are not fairly judged by them. However, since more careful account has been taken of the physical environment in which the children grow up, it has been possible to construct other scales which give the advantage to children living in the country.

What, then, makes up these types of behaviour to which we apply the general term of intelligence? What kind of structure do they have? What distinguishes them from automatic behaviour, such as is seen in animals? These questions cannot be answered on the level of individual differences: they have to be approached in a totally different perspective, that of mental functioning.

3 Defining intelligence

Thus far we have avoided defining intelligence. Binet, when asked what it was, replied jokingly 'Intelligence? It is what my test measures.' He was giving a scientist's operational definition, like the physicist who defined space by the instruments which measured it. However such a reply is an evasion; it is essential to have a definition if we are to study the emergence and development of intelligence in the child.

This is not as easy as it seems. Pierre Janet tells the story of a young nurse assigned to look after a rich and authoritarian old woman, who was completely irresponsible and had to be told what to do while given the impression that she was being obeyed. 'How do you expect me to deal with this situation?' asked the nurse. 'One of us has to give the orders, but you tell me not to contradict her!' Janet concluded that the young woman was obviously not intelligent. In other words she was not able to adapt to all the contradictory aspects of the situation; she could not use her discretion to ignore the *secondary* elements and concentrate on the *relevant* elements. Intelligent behaviour in this case appears as a complex link between situation and response, a 'something' which takes place inside the 'black box'. This 'black box' is the organism itself intervening between the totality of the stimuli impinging upon it (S) and the response which is elicited from it (R) – figure 18.

The advent of the computer has made it easier to state the question in these terms. Computers have an input through which they are supplied with information, and an output, generally a printing mechanism, through which they deliver their results. Inside the computer, between input and output, there must be a *program*, a set of rules for calculating or treating the data which has been drawn up by the programmer, translated into the appropriate code and fed in at the start.

In animals we know more or less what is inside the black box: innate programs to deal with most normal situations. Some of these programs – the *tropisms* – are very simple or are applicable to very simple organisms, while others – the *instincts* and *reflexes* – apply to organisms higher up the scale. The common element in all three cases is the fairly rigid link (with a certain range of individual variation, some species, such as the rat, showing less rigidity in this respect) between the stimuli and the responses, and the important fact that these links are not, essentially, forged in a period of learning within the individual history of the organism.

In the case of the tropism, the physico-chemical stimulus acts directly on the whole organism and causes the tropism, determining its direction and degree. With the instinct and the reflex, the stimulus *releases* a response already built into the organism as part of its heredity. The response may be considered one of the principles of the organism's biological functioning, both in its whole (instinct) and its parts (reflex).

In the past it was thought that it might be possible to reduce human behaviour – whatever that was – to these rigid behaviour patterns observed in animals. Loeb, who made a particular study of the tropism, thought that conjugal love could be explained as a complex set of tropisms of the same nature as the impulse that irresistibly attracts water-fleas to the light. La Mettrie (*L'Homme machine*, 1751) had already tried to reduce human behaviour to simple reflexes. His attempts were admittedly more literary and philosophical than scientific, but they were lent credibility by Pavlov's conditioned reflexes and by the ideological materialism of the Russian psychologists. McDougall, at the beginning of the century, put forward a theory of human behaviour which was based on instinctive conduct. However, when the rigid behaviour patterns of animals are applied to human beings this is always done by way of metaphor or analogy and always with the reservation that human behaviour is less rigid. Therefore it is difficult to see what is gained by the analogy and it seems preferable, whatever

18 (*left*) Intelligence may be thought of as a 'something', an intervening variable, between a set of stimuli (S) and the organism's response (R). This scheme presents the organism as a 'black box' whose functioning the psychologist must try to determine. (*right*) In the case of animals the 'black

$$S \Longleftarrow \boxed{?} \Longrightarrow R \qquad S \Longleftarrow \boxed{T/R/I/-} \Longrightarrow R$$

relationship may finally be established between human and animal behaviour (for ultimately man is an animal, however complex his behaviour may be), to define intelligent conduct in its own terms.

J.S. Bruner argues that man's evolution during the past five hundred thousand years has not been a morphological evolution, but is attributable to his use of external 'complementary systems', rather like the hermit crab's methods of protecting its stomach by covering it with various kinds of shells. These complementary systems are of three types: those which extend motor capacity (as in cutting something or being transported by a vehicle), those which extend sensory capacity (ranging from the visual signals of primitive societies to the radar in modern aircraft), and those which extend reasoning capacity (from primitive myths to modern systems of logic). These systems are culturally transmitted and relate to rules of functioning which are also of a collective nature; they involve the existence of some sort of internal organisation which facilitates their function and which might correspond to some hereditary potential, naturally selected in the course of generations by the elimination of those people who did not possess it.

In a very profound sense Man may be described as a species who has become specialised through his use of technical complements. His selection and survival have depended on a morphology and mental equipment capable of being related to the external systems that rendered his subsequent evolution possible.

We move, perceive and think, adds Bruner, in a way which depends more on our techniques than on the basic arrangement of connectors in our nervous system.

box' contains automatic behaviour, such as tropisms (T), reflexes (R) and instinctive behaviour (I) which account for the greater part of animal actions. Some species manifest a certain degree of acquired behaviour (habit), but this has relatively little importance in the totality of behaviour.

The nature of intelligence

It is these 'amplifiers of the rational capacities', then, which would form an important part of our intelligent behaviour and which profoundly distinguish it from the behaviour of animals. The symbol of this behaviour is language; not language as the expression of feelings (animals are capable of this – an example is the behaviour of a dog which wants to go for a walk), or as a set of social rituals (again animals are capable of this – the leader of a wolf pack can impose submission on an inferior simply by the way he looks at him), but language as a system of *representative* symbols and a set of *grammatical* rules. Broadly speaking, there are two main theories about the nature of this intelligence. Both theories are 'classical' in the sense that they have been elaborated in great detail by philosophical tradition and are still the subject of research and discussion today.

The first theory is based on the obvious similarity of very general mental categories in all human beings. In spite of minor variations due to differing cultures and histories there is a universal conception of space, time, perceptible objects, even of causality, or at least of whatever regulates our daily actions. These abstract ideas are universal because they are innate. This does not mean that they are part of everyone's mental equipment from the very beginning, but there are many other kinds of hereditary behaviour which only appear after a certain period of maturational delay: standing upright, language (the act of talking, not the handling of one particular language), sexual behaviour, parental behaviour. If this theory were correct the black box would contain inherited schemata, mental *gestalten*, 'innate' concepts. Intelligent behaviour would be very similar in structure to perceptual behaviour, and would refer to analogous 'laws', such as the principle of closure which makes us see a square in four suitably-placed dots and find the fourth proportional in a series of two proportions. Intelligent perception would be characterised by a particular feeling, the 'Eureka' which accompanies the discovery of the vital relationship or the solution to the problem. Kurt Koffka's excellent book on child psychology, published in 1921, has eloquently developed this thesis.

The idea that we inherit these intellectual structures or mental programs which enable us to deal with life more efficiently is apparently contradicted by the broadening of our cultural frames of reference and by the historical evolution of intellect. This is the basis of the second theory, which attributes everything to environment and thinks of the intellectual structures as mental habits, actions which have been learnt according to the universal laws of habit-formation and consolidated by the actual encounters of the organism with its environment. It is only within a restricted linguistic field that general mental categories appear to be similar; as soon as we go beyond these limits we find time, space and causality defined in totally different ways, and we also find totally different ways of expressing the most banal human experiences. (B. L. Whorf in particular has made much of this point and has provoked heated discussion in psycholinguistics.) History itself, within a single tradition such as Western culture, creates new ways of thought, produces new categories and invents new ideas in response to the new problems with which it challenges man. In France, Meyerson has become the advocate of this 'essential historicity' of the mind. However, it is the Anglo-Saxon psychologists, from Thorndike and Watson to Tolman, Skinner, Estes and Berlyne, who are particularly associated with this theory. They have contributed greatly to research on habit-formation and are the most impressive group working in experimental psychology, but they have a kind of fervour which often takes on the appearance of intransigent dogmatism.

These two rival theories have made a most important contribution to empirical knowledge. Both of them have provoked experiment, research and complementary theories, both have inspired professional dedication and loyalty. But the most productive and significant group working in this field of the origins of intelligence cannot be identified with either of the schools just mentioned. It boldly attempts to synthesise them, presenting the valuable and distinctive elements of each.

Piaget and the Geneva group

Jean Piaget was born in 1896 at Neuchâtel (Switzerland), and at an early age prepared himself for a scientific career. He took a Master of Science degree, and a doctorate in biology in 1918. For many years he was an eminent specialist in malacology (the science of molluscs) and by 1930 had written many articles on various aspects of this science. However, he did not regard scientific enquiry as an end in itself, but rather as an example of the way the mind acquires truths and uses them to find the truth itself. The problem of 'knowledge' soon became his principal interest.

His work in this respect falls into three main phases, the first being the exploration of mental function in the child – language, thought, representation of the world, moral judgment. He outlines his method for this. It consists of questioning the child, perhaps on an idea (where does the wind come from?), perhaps on an experiment (dissolving a piece of sugar in a glass of water and asking what has happened to it), but instead of considering only the child's answer, Piaget concentrates on the reasons given. It is clear that this method has to be very flexible, that it demands very strong structuring by the examiner to avoid any direct suggestion, and that it produces some kind of diagnosis of the thought-processes. Piaget appropriately called it a 'clinical method', by analogy with the method employed by the psychiatrist.

19 Jean Piaget (b. 1896).

The second phase is an ambitious study which takes the child at the beginning of his life and follows his mental development until he reaches adult intelligence. For this purpose Piaget first observed his own three children. He then enlarged his group of subjects and continued with increasingly systematic experiments, guided by hypotheses about the intellectual structures he was studying.

Thirdly, after the publication in 1947 of the *Psychology of Intelligence*, a phase of synthesis, recapitulation and systematic testing began, which resulted in 1955 in the creation of a Centre of Genetic Epistemology at Geneva. This brought together a team of specialists from various disciplines, working to yearly programmes which were discussed at meetings to which everyone whose opinion might be useful was invited. The published works of the centre already number more than twenty volumes.

The repercussions of this immense work – the major volumes (often collectively written) and nearly two hundred articles – have been somewhat erratic. This is shown by the different rate at which translation, particularly into English, has taken place. The works of the first phase were quickly disseminated and replaced by numerous studies the results of which did not always agree with

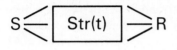

20 For Piaget, the 'black box' comprises intellectual structures which are a function of the individual's development stage – Str (t), where t = time.

those of Piaget. The works of the second phase have been confined largely to the French-speaking public, or at least to Continental circles. Then in about 1960 Piaget's work suddenly began to arouse interest in England and America and he enjoyed a sort of vogue, marked by the publication of general works like that of Flavell (1963) and by the devotion of whole symposia or seminars to the discussion of his principal ideas.

To return to the notation used above, Piaget's system may be symbolically represented by figure 20. Between the environmental stimuli and the response appear the structures (as in the gestalt conception), but these structures are a function of the organism's stage of evolution (they are a function of time, *t*), although in other respects they are not wholly determined by the action of the environment (as certain 'connectionist' theories claim). In this formulation there are three essential elements – *structure*, *stage* (state of a structure at any given moment) and *internal structuring*. Each of these will be discussed in detail.

The idea of structure

Few terms are so fashionable today as 'structure', whether in the abstract sciences such as mathematics, or in the empirical sciences such as psychology and sociology. But this popularity conceals a danger: the word has a precise meaning within each discipline, and yet the ideas represented are very different.

In the sense which concerns us, the idea of structure is related to two contexts, slightly different but each important. In the first place, the term 'structure' means 'the disposition of the parts of a whole, as distinct from their function' (Lalande's philosophical dictionary). Thus in biology it means the anatomical constitution as distinct from the physiological phenomena. When one talks of the structure of intelligence, therefore, one is distinguishing between the internal organisation and its functioning. This means that in defining precisely the function of intelligence one is, at least in part, defining its structure by contrast.

For Piaget, as for Bruner, intelligence is *adaptation*. Its function is to ensure the survival of the organism and thus the survival of the species. Like biological adaptation, it results from the interaction of internal and external factors. To start with the second, the action of the environment continually forces the organism to modify itself in order to go on existing (*accommodation*); in the animal world this modification takes visible forms, in man it affects the form of his thinking or the ways in which he knows things. But wherever it can, the organism also imposes its own forms on the environment: it modifies the environment in order to *assimilate* it. These processes of assimilation can be observed in the nucleus or the cell, and in the digestive processes, while in mental activity they take the form of perception, representation and concept-formation, and activities such as games or artistic creation. Actually, however, these two aspects of the organism's active adaptation to its environment are intimately bound together. All behaviour involves both of them simultaneously, tó varying degrees. But in so far as one aspect predominates over the other, the behaviour remains biased and unstable and swings back of its own accord to a more balanced state. This process underlies the dynamics of mental evolution in the child. As a starting point, this dynamic evolution may be thought of as a series of alternating phases where first assimilation, and then accommodation, predominate until they achieve balance in a harmonious unity. The very early days of life when the infant is little more than a digestive tract (assimilation) are followed by a period of active exploration when he strives to dominate the bewildering variety of stimuli in his environment (accommodation); through his play he tries to bend things and people to his will (assimilation), but by imitation, and a little later by his school work, he becomes open to outside influences (accommodation), and so the process continues.

If this were the functioning of intelligence, it would remain constant throughout the whole of evolution – a functional unity. However, this function occurs within the context of mental organisations which are themselves changing and developing. This is where the second meaning of 'structure' comes into play. The word is used to 'designate a whole, formed of interdependent phenomena (as opposed to a simple combination of elements), each of which relies on the others and can only be what it is within and by its relation to them' (Lalande). This immediately suggests the structure of the skeleton, each bone of which is dependent on all the others and can only be defined in terms of its location and its relationship with the others. With intelligence, then, what are the 'phenomena' which comprise the structure? If this question had been asked a century ago it would have received such answers as: 'intelligence resides in the combination of memory and attention', where the 'phenomena' comprising the structure would have been thought of as faculties, or as independent organs within the 'mental organisation'. The answer which Piaget gives is quite different: instead of harking back to the past it refers us to the latest developments in our technology. The 'phenomena' in the intellectual structure may be thought of as an algorithm.

The algorithm, which is a fundamental concept in the theory of modern computers, owes its name to an Arabian mathematician of the Middle Ages, Al Khowarazmi. Through the centuries it has been a favourite subject for speculation, notably in Leibniz's dream of discovering a 'universal algorithm' capable of solving any problem. An algorithm is a set of instructions which lead infallibly to the solution of a problem. One example among many could be Euclid's algorithm for finding the highest common factor of two numbers:

1 Take the two numbers, **a** and **b**.
2 Compare the two numbers.
3 If the two numbers compared are equal, they are equal to the desired result. The calculation is completed. If not, go on to the next step.
4 Subtract the smaller of the two numbers from the larger. Replace the larger number by the difference thus obtained. Go back to step 2.

Suppose we want to find the highest common factor of 18 and 12. The procedure would be as follows. Step 1: 18 and 12. Step 2: compare 18 and 12. Step 3: the two numbers are not equal, so Step 4 must be taken. Subtract 12 from $18 = 6$, replace 18 by 6, compare the two numbers 12 and 6, subtract one from the other $= 6$, replace 12 by 6. According to Step 3 (the numbers are now equal), 6 is the desired result.

With intellectual evolution the problem is to decide which sets of rules apply to mental function. Piaget's central thesis is that these sets of rules do not remain constant throughout mental development, but are modified with age and may therefore be divided into successive stages comparable to different algorithms or programs in a computer – or rather in four different and increasingly complex types of computer.

The notion of stages

Mlle Inhelder, who worked with Piaget for many years and has recently expounded his ideas, defines the stage by four criteria:

1 Each stage involves a period of formation (genesis) and a period of attainment. Attainment is characterised by the progressive organisation of a composite structure of mental operations.

2 Each structure constitutes at the same time the attainment of one stage and the starting point of the next stage of a new evolutionary process.
3 The order of succession of the stages is constant. Age of attainment can vary within certain limits as a function of factors of motivation, exercise, cultural milieu and so forth.
4 The transition from an earlier stage to a later stage follows a law of implication analogous to the process of integration, preceding structures becoming a part of later structures.

The number of principal stages varies slightly in Piaget's works, largely according to how detailed an account is given. (There are fewer stages when development is surveyed as a whole and more when the subject is dealt with more thoroughly and reference is made to particular aspects – rather like the features on maps covering regions of varying size.) This account is based on that given by Mlle Inhelder.

Stage 1 Sensori-motor operations This stage corresponds roughly to the first eighteen months of life. It facilitates the progressive building-up of the world of objects, the sensori-motor construction of the immediate environment.

This period of development is divided into six sub-stages. At first the infant is only capable of reflex activity, responses he has inherited which are automatically released by an external signal and only involve one part of his organism. An example is the sucking reflex, which Preyer (the first systematic observer of infantile behaviour) was already carefully studying at the end of the last century. In the second sub-stage these various reflex activities are modified through actual experience and begin to be co-ordinated. The infant is now about four months old. In the third sub-stage, at about eight months, the infant begins to attribute a certain perman-ence to objects; he directs his gaze and sometimes his actions towards them. In the next sub-stage these actions become more

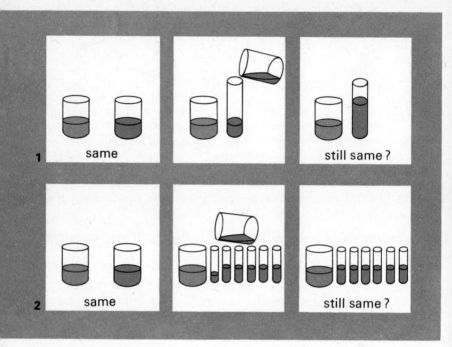

precise and intentional, and make use of a primitive principle of causality, or relationship between cause and effect. What has been learned begins to be applied, and certain types of behaviour are repeated. In the fifth sub-stage, between twelve and eighteen months, the child begins to act systematically towards his surroundings, he looks for new solutions and appreciates novelty. Finally in the sixth sub-stage the early forms of symbolic representation appear, together with the first signs that the baby is systematically looking for solutions rather than proceeding by trial and error.

Stage 2 Concrete operations From two to seven years of age mental operations become more elaborate. They take as long a period again – until eleven or twelve years – to complete their structure and refinement.

It is in his study of this stage that Piaget has made his biggest

21 In this Piaget experiment, the child is told that the containers hold the same volume of liquid. In line 1 the liquid from one container is poured, in front of the child, into a longer but narrower tube. Before a certain stage of maturity, the child does not recognise conservation of quantity. He thinks there is less liquid because the tube is narrower, or more because it is longer. Line 2 shows a variant.

contribution to our understanding of the child's mental functioning. At the beginning, concrete operations are irreversible for the child; this is shown by the fact that the child does not anticipate their result and is guided by perceptual evidence. Gradually the operations do become reversible, and thenceforth form a system which is analogous to an algorithm.

To take a more striking example – the child has in front of him two balls of plasticine which he knows are the same size. He is told to roll one of them into a long sausage, or make it into a cake, or to break it up into small pieces. Each time he does this he is asked if the plasticine is still 'the same', if it has got bigger or smaller or has remained the same amount. Most children of five or six years say without hesitation that the plasticine has not stayed the same throughout its transformations, but has got bigger or smaller according to its visual appearance. Only after a long period of preparation can the child grasp the principle of invariance when the ball of plasticine is reconstructed out of the sausage or the small separate pieces in order to prove that the quantity of material has not altered. These 'invariances' are established at different times according to what they refer to; there is a sub-stage where the conservation of substance is established, but not of weight, then a further sub-stage when the conservation of substance and weight is established, but not of volume, and so on. The intellectual operations become progressively more elaborate, and finally form logical–mathematical structures which, when internalised and freed from their concrete content, will constitute the formal operations of the next stage.

Stage 3 Formal operations In the third stage the thought-processes of the child begin to resemble those of the adolescent and adult. From now on it is possible to form hypotheses and reason 'in the abstract'. We have mentioned the case of the American boy who

22 Another device of Piaget's : the lines represent tests of increasing difficulty, which will not be performed correctly until the child's intelligence has reached the stage of concrete operations. The pouring is done behind a screen, and the child is then required to mark with a line its guess at the new level of liquid. The screen is then removed, and guess is compared with result.

was asked problems of simple arithmetic and refused to do the sum because it referred to something which in his experience was impossible. He had not reached the third stage. This stage is also distinguished by a new – systematic – way of thinking in the solution of fairly complex problems.

As an example let us imagine a group of five bottles filled with colourless liquid. The first, third and fifth, when mixed, will produce a brown liquid. The fourth bottle contains a reducing agent and the second is neutral. The problem is to combine the contents of the bottles in such a way as to produce the brown liquid. The child at the previous stage will experiment without any precise plan. The adolescent, on the other hand, will proceed by deductive hypotheses, trying all the combinations in turn in a planned sequence which guarantees that he will achieve the desired result.

What is important here is the successive approximation to the formal models of logic, and the mastery of the intellectual measures through which modern science continually extends its knowledge.

The internal structuring

How can this successive approximation be explained? Those who believe it is innate solve the problem by resorting to heredity or to structures of a perceptual kind. For the advocates of environment, these developing abilities are the result of cultural influences. From birth to adolescence, the child does nothing but internalise the thought-models which have been elaborated by philosophers for centuries, and the mistakes to which Piaget drew attention are only sporadic and marginal failures in assimilation.

Piaget takes a third view. He is too well versed in scientific history not to be on his guard against attributing too much importance to heredity. However, he is also too much of a logician and mathematician to underestimate the difficulty of deriving

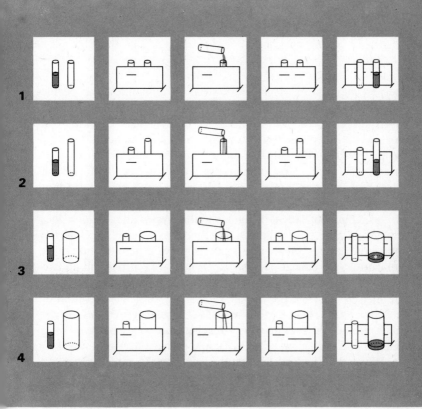

complex structures from the environment. There may be things which go in pairs, but the number *two* does not exist in nature. We impose it on what we perceive, to make it more orderly and manageable.

The mainspring of intellectual evolution, in Piaget's view, is the interaction of the mental processes and the environment. The intellectual structures are formed by a kind of internal necessity, such as the balancing of the conflicting tendencies of assimilation and accommodation. This solution has its difficulties, and people have not been slow to point them out. Controlled experiments have nevertheless shown that the intellectual structures develop to a great extent independently of the cultural environment, in that they are observed in virtually the same sequence in children of very different cultural backgrounds (the study carried out in Hong Kong by Goodnow, on boys aged 10, 11, 12 and 13, showed that the principle of conservation of weight and volume was independent of IQ but dependent on age), and that systematic teaching does not have stable results unless the child has already reached the appropriate stage. Smedlund's study is relevant here because of its implications for education. The experiment was carried out on two groups of subjects aged from five to seven. The first group, comprising thirteen children, had reached the stage where conservation of substance had been established. The second group, of eleven children, had not spontaneously reached this stage, but they were coached and pushed on until they could manage it. A trap was then set. When they had all apparently acquired the same concepts a trick experiment was proposed. In changing the shape of the ball of plasticine the examiner secretly removed a piece so that the substance was not conserved. Six of the thirteen subjects in the 'mature' group resisted the falsified perceptual evidence: a piece of plasticine 'must' be missing, they said – it fell off, the examiner took it. Of the subjects who had only been taught conservation, none 'resisted' and all of them happily reverted to the 'explanations' they had given spontaneously before the period of training.

Does this mean that mental development takes place in the void, like physical maturation which always, at least in normal circumstances, progresses towards adult stature? Not at all, because adaptation proceeds under the pressure of the environment, even though it does not owe its final structure to this environment. Bruner insists on this point:

The logical structures become more elaborate in order to support new forms of relationship with the external world. It is obvious that the child at the pre-operational stage, protected by his parents, does not need to manipulate the world of objects unaided until a certain pressure is put upon him to be independent. This is the moment when the concrete operations emerge. Similarly, the child at the stage of concrete operations does not need to manipulate the world of facts (except in imagination) until he is subjected to another new pressure; the formal operations then supervene on his thought-processes and will soon characterise them.

But if the child is subjected to pressures in this way, he also desires to escape from them; he is pushed forward by his basic drives. This is a second aspect of mental activity, and it marks the second phase in modern child psychology.

4 The basic drives

Child psychology did not take a serious interest in the subject of 'drives' or basic motives until after the Second World War, and people today still find it difficult to understand that children differ so greatly from adults in their motives. There is also a tendency to simplify the problem, not only in childhood but also in maturity and old age. This simplification consists mainly in recognising only the drives of which we are aware. Yet clearly we are not conscious of all our drives or even of all the most important ones.

In earlier societies – primitive communities and even in the early stages of industrial society – the chief concern of most people was to ensure the satisfaction of their basic biological needs: food, clothing, shelter from the cold and damp, having a family and if possible bringing it up. All available energy went into the struggle for survival.

However, in circumstances where people could eat their fill without worry, these basic biological needs began to be satisfied so easily that people were able literally to 'think about other things'. Since motivation could no longer be obviously reduced to a list of elementary needs, a 'theory' of human motivation became necessary.

The first attempt to analyse motivation gave the child the same motivations as the adult. This seemed so natural that no one suspected the problems it would raise. As La Bruyère wrote:

Children are haughty, disdainful, quick-tempered, envious, curious, selfish, lazy, fickle, timid, intemperate, liars, dissimulators; they laugh and cry easily; they experience immoderate joy and bitter sorrow over very small things; they do not like pain but enjoy inflicting it: they are already men.

Not everyone of course was so pessimistic about childhood; since the Romantic era it had been consciously idealised. The general idea however was the same: one moved from the adult to the child by subtraction; the child had the same motivations as the adult, but they were fewer (physical growth and of course sexual maturity would add some other motivations later) and were less powerful.

Freud and childhood

It was this implicit belief that caused the horrified reaction to psychoanalysis. Sigmund Freud was born in 1856. He grew up in Vienna when it was a brilliant European capital, the centre of a great empire. He studied medicine there and embarked on a career as a neurologist which would have led him to a university lectureship. But he realised that it was an unpromising path and that a junior research post would not enable him to bring up a family. He turned to private practice in the field closest to his previous interests. He completed his training in Paris under Charcot and at Lille under Bernheim, the one a specialist in hysteria, the other a specialist in hypnosis. Then with some knowledge of the new illnesses of the time – the neuroses – and of the new techniques, he began to explore the different kinds of abnormal or inappropriate behaviour. The turn of the century was a turning-point also for Freud. He was forty-four years old and had already established a reputation in neurology; he now began a fresh scientific career, publishing *The Interpretation of Dreams*, which laid down the principles of psychoanalysis. In 1904 he published *The Psychopathology of Everyday Life*, and in 1906 his *Introduction to Psychoanalysis*. After the First World War he revised his theories extensively (without managing to take all his early disciples with him), distinguishing an essential duality in the human organism which causes it to be torn between an impulse towards life (*Eros* or *libido*) and an impulse towards death (*Thanatos* or *destrudo*). He was now over sixty, and had become the grave, inscrutable man of his last portraits. In 1923, with a cancer of the jaw for which he had nearly thirty operations, he entered a prolonged period of suffering further darkened in 1938 by exile. He died in London in September 1939.

It was because Freud was an astute neurologist that he was intrigued by hysterical behaviour: such behaviour was 'impossible' in the sense that it did not obey the laws of anatomy or physiology, but only related to what the subject himself knew – or imagined – about his nervous system. Thus there were certain cases of blindness or partial paralysis without any organic damage. Medicine had made rapid progress since the theory was formulated in 1850 that all disease represented damage to a tissue or a group of cells. In hysteria, one was confronted with a disease which caused undeniable suffering to its victims, but had no organic cause. The cause must therefore be psychological. But the sufferer was not consciously aware of it. The implication was a theoretical absurdity – an *un*conscious mental phenomenon when scientific psychology from its earliest days had defined the mental by the conscious. Furthermore, this mental phenomenon had all the appearances of a force, a drive. This brings us back to a scheme which served in the previous chapter to clarify intelligent behaviour, but this time what is inside the 'black box' is not an intellectual but a dynamic structure (figure 24). This arrangement is partly a set of signals or stimuli which constitute the situation of the organism, and partly behaviour. To relate these two groups of observable data, to make the behaviour intelligible in terms of the signals which release it, we endow the organism with unobservable data; the drives. Freud's great contribution lay in his refusal to accept the drives of which we are consciously aware as the connecting point, but in taking them as forms of behaviour which had to be explained in themselves or which were connected with things not observable.

Freud began exploring the conscious (the flux of images and 'ideas' about which his patients could talk to him) first by means of hypnosis (or induced sleep creating a relationship between the

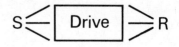

subject and his hypnotist), and later through free association, and traced his way back through his patient's history until he was faced with motivations and attitudes which he could only approach through the child that his adult patient once was. But it was a completely different child from the traditional picture accepted by the adult. This child was not a miniature adult but a totally different being. Nor was he innocent, but a creature obstinately bent on his own satisfaction, a kind of powerful, cruel force, ready to smash everything in his pursuit of gratification, enslaving others or becoming their slave, according to his particular inclinations, outside time, outside reality, more a thing than a person, and bound at some deep level to the life force itself. Freud himself found it difficult to accept this picture of the child, in such violent contrast with the sentimental views of the period and seemingly both shocking and improbable. But he then turned to questioning the reasons for his surprise. Why was he shocked by this revelation of childhood dominated by the need for pleasure and satisfaction? Obviously because he would have to apply to himself what he discovered in his patients, and admit that once, in his distant past, before he became a rational being with acceptable motivations, he had been the same self-willed creature bent only on his own satisfaction. But he no longer had any direct memory of this strange existence. Why?

Freud's answer inaugurated a new era in psychology. It had of course been noted before that we forget many things and remember only certain things. Attempts had been made to study memory, since the way in which an idea was engraved on the mind, retained and re-mobilised, seemed to merit explanation. Freud suggested that it might be more important to explain forgetting, which our everyday experience shows is the result of some degree of conflict between rival motivations. However, as a general rule it is other people's behaviour that we are able to interpret in terms of these conflicts, which we perceive with remarkable shrewdness and to the considerable embarrassment of the people concerned. Freud invites us to see ourselves with the eyes of others, to see in ourselves the 'other' which we are without knowing it. And in the first place to see why we see this other so dimly. What are the forces which repress our memory of the 'other' which we were in childhood?

According to Freud, these forces are a certain idea of our self which conforms to the prevailing social standards of what a 'good' adult ought to be, and which may thus be interpreted as an internalisation of the social norm. The idea of childhood, which is pushed out of the consciousness by this 'conscience', is necessarily incompatible with it, and is therefore on moral grounds rejected, repudiated, and repressed. It is thus not surprising that we cannot get back to our childhood, since the whole of our adult adaptation to life rests on the active forgetting of this childhood.

What is dangerous to our adult adaptation in this rejected childhood?

The answer is: drives, which, if they were still directing our behaviour, would bring us into conflict with the social norms. Certain adults do reveal these drives in spite of social prohibitions. We call such people 'perverse' because they derive satisfaction from behaviour which most adults reject with horror. Freud discovered a link between these 'failures in socialisation' and the subject's childhood; perverts are people who are not wholly adult; in their drives they have retained something which is appropriate to the child. This means that the child is naturally perverse, in the sense that he presents as a natural trait behaviour which is culpable in the adult. In addition, he is a complete repertoire of all perversions – a 'polymorphic pervert' – but he is forced by his development to abandon perverse sources of satisfaction in order to attain different, adult forms of behaviour. Is it possible to enumerate these repressed drives? Freud strove to do so, and the psychoanalytic school has continued his inventory, sometimes to rather excessive lengths. We shall go briefly through the evolutionary stages of the drives as set out by E. H. Erikson, with the schemata which illustrate them. As in Erikson, the account will be simplified to describe only the evolution which takes place in boys.

The 'oral-respiratory-sensory' stage At first the infant lives and expresses love with his mouth. It has often been said that the baby starts life in the form of a digestive tube open at both ends. Psychoanalysis adds that this state is linked to the first satisfaction of a sexual nature – that is to say, there is a continuity between this satisfaction and that which the adult will later derive from his sexual activity, much as there is between the seed and the fully-grown plant. The first behaviour-type in the baby consists of passive incorporation (figure 25). If at this stage the baby does not encounter any systematic deprivation (provoking frustration), he will develop a sense of well-being and security which will form the basis of his personality.

From this stage onwards an external element, the person who satisfies the baby's basic needs, plays a vital role. In most societies the role goes to the natural mother, sometimes to a nurse, or in certain cases to maternal substitutes such as a grandmother. Thus in this primary stage the baby is brought into contact with an external 'object' through which he obtains satisfaction.

The 'oral-incorporative' stage Satisfaction is still obtained through the mouth (whence the term 'oral' in the designation of this stage), but incorporation becomes more active; the mouth closes over the breast where the baby sucks the nipple. This behaviour-type is henceforth an active 'taking', an attacking, tearing action. It is made possible by the maturation of the bones of the jaw, which make the infant's bite progressively more effective. It also makes it

25 The first stage of Erikson's schema : at the 'oral-respiratory-sensory' stage behaviour focusses on the oral zone (a), while the other zones (anal – b, genital – c) are still latent. Behaviour is primarily incorporative (shown by the arrow entering the cavity open to receive it). Other modes are subordinated ; they will become important in later stages. At this stage, the baby lives and expresses love with his mouth.

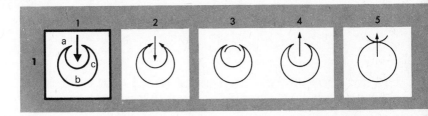

more painful for the mother when she continues to breast-feed the child. The baby obscurely senses the movement of withdrawal he provokes, and has an intuition of the cause. Thus he experiences his first feeling of 'evil', says Erikson, the basis of his knowledge of wrong (figure 26).

The 'anal-urethral-muscular' stage   The dominant zone now changes. In the preceding stages it was the mouth; it now passes to the other extremity of the alimentary canal, to the excretory zone. Here the infant is confronted with social necessities, at least within our society, and particularly within the middle class, which has furnished the standards of society since the Industrial Revolution. The child must learn both to restrain himself throughout the period when those around him expect him to be 'good', and to let himself go when social circumstances allow it, when he is sitting on his pot or in whatever situation society provides for the elimination of excrement. If this phase is smoothly passed through, the child will have laid a firm foundation for his subsequent independence; if he encounters major difficulties, he will be troubled by feelings of doubt and shame (figure 27).

Here as in earlier stages the central object in the child's life is his mother (or her substitute). It is usually for her that he exercises his new muscular powers, and to her that he makes the gift of these precious materials to which adults obviously attach a special value.

26 (*top*) When the second of Erikson's stages, known as the 'oral-incorporative' stage, is added, the mouth is still the dominant zone but the mode of behaviour changes. It is now an active 'taking'; the baby bites and tears. The earlier behaviour continues to subsist, but is subordinated, and more advanced behaviour begins to suggest itself.

27 (*bottom*) With the third stage, 'anal-urethral-muscular', a new zone becomes dominant. This is the excretory zone, 'b' in figure 25. The child has to learn to control his bowels as society demands; he must 'hold on' (column 3) for as long as is necessary, and 'let go' (column 4) when the right moment arrives. Earlier behaviour continues to subsist, and the child regresses to it when he encounters difficulties in his latest task.

For a long time avarice has been connected with constipation in the popular mind. In a way, psychoanalysis takes seriously what had only seemed a joke or a playful analogy. In the Middle Ages it was popularly believed that the Devil turned the gold which he gave his victims into excrement; now psychoanalysis has interpreted the metaphors of the myth on a serious level.

The 'locomotor and infantile genital' stage The child now emerges from the narrow circle of his home. He mixes with his 'peers' (his playmates), and begins to make a way for himself, he has battles with objects and he learns to handle language in manipulating things. His behaviour-type is now active intrusion, emphasised by the term 'locomotor' in the designation of this stage. However, the dominant zone has changed once more. From now onwards it is genital, in the true sense (figure 28). This does not mean that a child of this age, from three to five or six years, only engages in genital activity. Obviously this is not so. Yet it may be said that the kind of behaviour (intrusion) manifested in this zone is found in all his activities, which are therefore coloured by it. He reacts boisterously

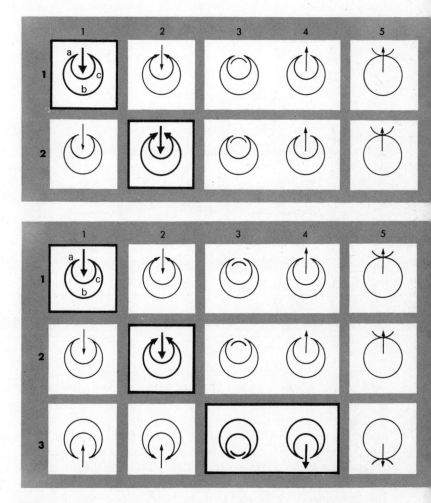

28 At the fourth stage, 'locomotor and infantile genital', the genital zone with its conduct of masculine intrusion and feminine incorporation (M and F on the fifth line) becomes dominant. After this the course of infantile sexual development undergoes a dramatic change. The child (here assumed to be a boy) comes face to face with the barrier of incest, and generally rejects (by actively forgetting it) the desire he has for his mother.

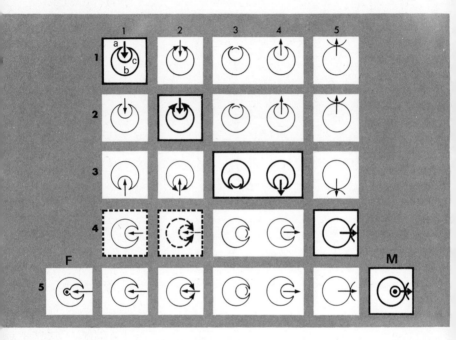

to things, shouts, and is aggressive. Erikson's scheme explains this by retaining all the acquired forms of behaviour at each stage but giving dominance to one at the time of its evolution (this is shown by a heavy line in the diagrams).

At this stage a decisive change occurs. Until now the child strengthened his relationship with his mother at each successive stage. She was the central object of the oral stage in the two aspects defined above. She was the primordial 'other' in the anal stage, the one he sought to please and to present with gifts. In this new stage she continues to be the child's central objective, but with the change of zone, the child's behaviour creates a problem: his mother cannot be involved in his genital activity. The barrier of incest raises itself before the child: his mother is forbidden. The child also finds himself abruptly in rivalry with a powerful competitor, his father, who is already occupying the place the child wants to assume. Thus he enters into a triangular relationship which will cause him much painful conflict. On the one hand he is denied the satisfaction of his desires. But because this deprivation involves real anguish and causes the child to doubt himself, it will quickly become frustration, and the child will soon be trying to escape from the situation instead of continuing to hanker after his first objective.

The Oedipus complex is one of Freud's greatest discoveries. Once again, he was the first to be stunned by the implications of its importance in his own life. This cardinal point of psychoanalysis was not deliberately thought up – it forced itself on Freud as a hypothesis which gave reason and consistency to the behaviour his patients presented, and which had also arranged his own life as he now newly understood it. This 'first disappointment in love', as one of his earliest disciples called it, also explains why the child forgets his childhood as soon as he grows up. It is the Oedipus complex above all which provokes the rejection of childhood, because it is miserable, humiliating (like all disappointed love) and irremediable. It is tinged with resentment, the bitterness of the fox with the sour grapes.

This first drama is resolved when the child is obliged to renounce for some time all true genital activity and turn to the external world, where he will find the strength with which he sees his rival, his father, endowed. Hence the next stage.

The latency period For a number of years the child is 'out of the running', in a kind of hibernation which is in complete contrast to the intensity of his previous sexual conduct. This does not mean that he renounces all activity. On the contrary, he exhausts his energies in the conquest of the material world. He is sustained by his effort to identify with his father or with the adults – frequently his teachers – who fill this role towards him. He progresses from the material world to the world of relationships and symbols. His dominant behaviour is expressed in a great variety of action, and if he manages this stage smoothly he will establish an idea of his self which will protect him from feelings of inferiority. Freud considers this stage to be ultimately negative. There no longer seems to be a central 'object', a privileged Other, in the child's world. Admittedly the previous attachments remain, but the rejection of the Oedipus complex robs them of their power. Friendship and companionship are centred more on group activities than on individual people. For several years, before he is swept off his feet by the tumult of adolescence, the child appears to be in emotional harmony with his environment; he is self-sufficient, and he pursues his path peacefully and securely.

Adolescence In the evolution of the drives, adolescence represents the achievement of adult drives marked by secondary sexuality. The closed world of the latency period now opens, but this time on to an Other who is not explicitly part of the family structure, who is not forbidden by the barrier of incest, and with whom it is biologically possible to create a family, and in human terms a relationship where give and take are balanced and the happiness of each person depends on the fulfilment of both. The tension set up by repression will gradually dissolve (dissolution of the Oedipus complex), and if he is normal, that is to say perfectly adult, the young person will become an active member of the community, balancing his obligations against his rights as he mixes in the various circles which make up his human environment.

Psychoanalysis is without doubt the scientific approach which has provoked the most discussion and inspired the most research, and it has created a profound division of opinion between those who stubbornly reject everything tainted with Freudianism and those who see in it the only coherent formulation yet advanced to explain the internal evolution of personality.

The first Freudian hypothesis to raise difficulties was the revelation of infantile sexuality. Freud was bitterly attacked for his pansexualism. Curiously enough this is probably the area in which he has gained his clearest victory, at least in the minds of most people today, if not in the eyes of all scientists. In comparison with the last century, our age is marked by a freedom of discussion and even by a degree of license in private life which have restored sexuality to an important place in man's image of himself. We have in fact become so sexually conscious that it is sometimes necessary to recall that man has other capacities and does not simply exist from the waist down. This recognition of sexuality, however, has not completely swamped childhood. It is difficult for many psychologists to accept a perfect continuity between the various stages, as if they were reincarnations of the same force, and these prefer to think of the different stages as the successive emergence of different systems of drive, relatively independent of each other, and each carrying its own drives which mingle with and shade into the others, without either being absorbed completely by other drives or continuing completely intact, even when they reappear in the adult in the form of perversity or abnormality.

The second Freudian hypothesis has attracted more support, considering all the qualifications attached to the first one. Since Freud, tremendous importance has been attached to the early days of life. The circumstances of birth, the way in which the child is fed, and then weaned if he was breast-fed, the attitude of those around him towards cleanliness, aggression, and dependence – all this now has to be taken into account as being relevant both to the development of the individual and to the formation of distinctive cultural traits, particularly in primitive societies.

It is in research projects, however, that psychoanalysis has been especially productive. Supporters and critics of Freud have argued over the plausibility of Freudian claims, and have then gone on to carry out research studies which bristle with proofs and experimental results.

Freud had arrived at his 'system' through his interviews with maladjusted or actually sick adults. It was to explain their adult behaviour that he postulated an infantile development which linked together the stages he observed as a clinician. He himself had hardly made any direct observation of children. His own had already reached an advanced age when he elaborated his ideas, and he had rapidly become so absorbed in drafting his works and by his patients that his great work on psychoanalysis was finally founded on little more than two hundred cases, among whom children, in the main, were only included by accident. Do 'psychological laws' established in such circumstances have any value? At the very least they must be confirmed by direct observation and systematic experiment.

More and more direct studies have been made in the field of cultural anthropology. For about a hundred years efforts have been made to describe the differences which distinguish societies. However, among the host of characteristics which would make it possible to classify these differences it has not always been easy to distinguish between cause and effect. Psychoanalysis promises a better mode of classification. The relations of the child to his parents or to other adults in his environment have been taken as starting-points. Cultures (such as that of the Arapesh in the South Sea Islands, studied by Margaret Mead) have been found where the educational stress tends to consolidate or prolong the first Freudian stage in the development of drives. In this culture the adult is at

29 Certain primitive societies are thought by some to prolong the first Freudian stage in the development of drives. The mother is at the mercy of her child and cannot leave it for a moment.

the baby's service: the mother is always present, attentive to the baby's smallest signs, offering him the breast before he could possibly be hungry. Both parents are involved in the provision of food, and the whole society revolves round agrarian rites. The people are docile and gentle, not anxious to compete with each other, and reluctant to assume the responsibilities of authority. In other cultures the accent is on taking, the second Freudian stage, or else on holding and letting go (Western society seems to accord particular respect to the kind of behaviour which Freud termed 'anal' – the hoarding of possessions is dignified by the name of thrift or investment, the squandering of goods is commended as generosity, mere consumption is held up as an aim of social activity). Other cultures again revolve around aggression, and some are excessively puritanical in that they push everything to do with sex behind a barricade of prohibitions.

It is an achievement in itself that Freudian analysis furnished a conceptual basis for ethnology and provided a clear orientation for 'natural' observations. However, such observations will often lack rigour. The observer selects the traits which seem important to him, projecting into the culture he is observing the theory he wants to prove, and finds at the end only what he introduced at the beginning. The studies therefore must become more rigidly controlled, and subject to broader comparisons. Thus Whiting and Child studied the educational procedures in over eighty societies, relating educational practices to certain cultural traits such as the conception of illness and death. Here again, however, only fairly low correlations were found – a sure indication that there were considerable errors of observation and that the number of determinants was not fixed.

The Freudian view must not only be able to formulate intercultural comparisons. It must also be valid within a single culture – Western society, for example. In this area controlled studies have multiplied. It would be possible to take the stages one by one, and show how Freudian theory has stimulated research, and also how the results have frequently been misleading. Sewell and Mussen studied rigorously 161 subjects. With the aid of one of the best personality questionnaires available, they interviewed the children's teachers (to judge the children's independence, emotional control and acceptance of authority) and their mothers (on their nervous habits, speech difficulties, sensitivity and fears). According to the Freudian view, a certain number of traits would depend on circumstances of very early infancy, such as the method of feeding and the time of weaning. None of these predictions was fulfilled. The relationships which emerged did not conform to the theoretical expectations. However, it was possible to regroup the personality traits as Freud had suggested, into oral and anal. But these traits did not correspond to the evolutionary stage which gives them their name. Freud's clinical insight was confirmed, but often the determinants he had postulated to explain his observations were not the

30 A child (C) wants an object (G, goal) which is behind a barrier (B). Simply by its existence, this barrier acquires a negative force which repulses the child.

83

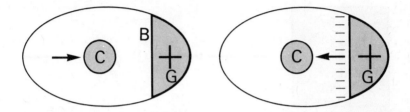

correct ones. In this sense it can be said that we enter modern child psychology through psychoanalysis, but we cannot continue in it there. This is also apparent from two points which were closely linked to the Freudian conception but rapidly acquired a certain independence.

Related motivational concepts

1 Frustration The first concerns a phenomenon to which we have already referred: frustration. This is a currently fashionable idea, but is none the clearer for that. We know that frustration is what occurs when an organism does not immediately manage to satisfy a need of some kind. However, there are varieties of frustration. First of all, following Lewin's convenient scheme, there is the simple situation shown in figure 30. The organism (for instance a child who wants to get at a sweet) is separated from his goal by a *barrier* (the sweet is out of reach): this is a situation of deprivation. In ordinary circumstances, deprivation inspires us to redouble our efforts (the child jumps higher, or goes and looks for a stool), and this is often enough to surmount the barrier. We approach our goal, take the object and consume it; our need is satisfied, and with its satisfaction we return to a state of neutrality. When the child has had several sweets he turns away from the one still left on the table.

This simple situation of deprivation is often termed frustration.

31 Here the child wants to climb a tree (T), but the goal, while desirable (+), is also dangerous (−) ; the child is caught in a field of conflicting forces and is therefore a prey to uncertainty. If in addition the goal is felt to be important, the situation will give rise to feelings of anguish and panic, which will release new kinds of behaviour.

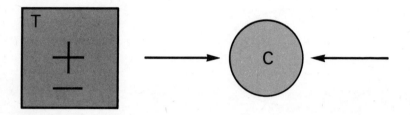

It is better to use this word only when two further conditions are present: first when the barrier is *resistant*, so that in spite of renewed efforts the organism remains deprived for some time, and second when, although the organism can survive without the need being satisfied (obviously it could not be deprived of air for long, nor could it manage for any long period without solid or liquid nourishment, sleep or activity), the need is still *important*.

The resistance of the barrier gives rise to a state of uncertainty. The organism is not capable of the action which would resolve the situation, and the combination of uncertainty and the importance of the goal provokes an internal state which is expressed in such terms as 'anxiety', 'panic', 'distress'. This is translated into behaviour by types of conduct which are either new or at least not habitual in easily-resolved situations – stamping one's feet, biting one's nails, pacing up and down, breaking ornaments, abusing the people present.

Thus an element is added between deprivation and frustration: the element of anxiety. This element becomes an objective in itself, but a negative one, in that from now on the organism seeks not so much to attain its original goal as to escape from anguish. It is in this sense that Maier talks of behaviour without a goal. The way in which the organism avoids anxiety constitutes a basic strategy, which will lay the foundation of its character.

The Freudian conception requires that in the course of his

development the child must necessarily be frustrated. In the fourth stage he cannot satisfy his need to possess his mother sexually. The stronger the need, the greater the frustration will be, particularly as the need has been reinforced in each of the earlier stages and will thus be more strongly disappointed in this new phase.

The earliest strategy which will resolve this insoluble problem is to 'opt out', to suppress the absence of a solution by suppressing the problem. This is the root of all repression: erasing the troublesome situation from the consciousness by consigning the drive which provoked it to the depths of oblivion.

Secondly, the organism may choose various forms of *aggression*. Experiment has shown that an embarrassing situation causes aggression. People have been asked for instance to solve a problem which could not be solved in the way demanded, such as placing a flower-pot on a chest of drawers from a distance, without moving one's feet outside a circle drawn on the ground, or finding the way through a maze from which there is no exit. After several fruitless attempts the unfortunate subjects who were given the tests turned either to abusing the tester ('The only thing these psychologists know how to do is invent things' – extro-punitive reaction), or to self-denigration ('Well, it's something I've never been able to do' – intro-punitive reaction) or to denying the importance of the task ('Anyway, what is the point of solving this problem?' – impunitive reaction). Rosenweig has constructed an interesting personality test on these observations, showing the habitual strategy used by an individual in a frustrating situation. In Freudian terms all such situations evoking these habitual strategies are said to be repetitions of the first frustrating situation in which our character was formed.

Aggression is not the only type of behaviour shown in response to a resistant barrier. Freud introduced a supplementary mechanism, *regression*, at this point. The frustrated organism regresses to

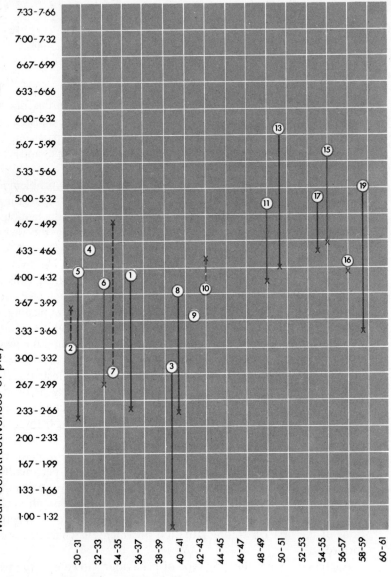

Mean constructiveness of play

Mental age in month.

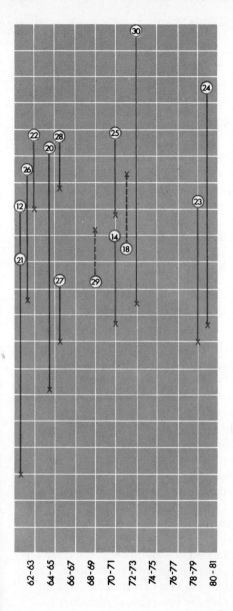

32 This diagram summarises the results of the most important experimental research carried out on the effects of *frustration*. At the first stage, each child was given a score for 'constructiveness' (shown by the position of the circle) according to what he did with the toys that were given him. The child was then subjected to a marked degree of frustration, after which the first step was repeated and his performance scored according to the same rules. All but three of the children (numbers 2, 7 and 18) showed a considerable drop in constructiveness; they *regressed* to a mode of behaviour which they had left behind. This regression is sometimes extremely marked (numbers 30, 24, 21, 3 and 23) and corresponds to a drop of several months in mental age; number 30, who obtained the highest score before frustration, dropped back to the score obtained by the youngest subjects, numbers 1 to 10.

forms of behaviour which were 'normal' at an earlier stage because they served to adapt the child to frustration, but which are now out of date. This explanation overlaps partly with the first one; there is a history of aggression. As the child grows up he disciplines his attacks, passing from a physical type of aggression to a more refined, verbal type, or to the subtlest type, passive aggression, which consists of ignoring or turning a deaf ear to his attacker. We should then observe a degraded form of aggression, reduced from its most advanced to its crudest form. However there are forms of behaviour other than aggression which are linked to previous stages in the evolution of drives. The child who is frustrated starts to suck his thumb.

These forecasts have been partly confirmed by experiment. But it was soon realised that a certain circularity occurred: one predicted aggression when one saw frustration, and then one induced frustration when one saw aggression, so that the consequence (aggression) was often the only evidence of the antecedent (frustration). There has also been some difficulty in reducing the observed behaviour to a unity. Aggression is not a uniform behaviour-type; it always has different shades and different determinants, and nothing is gained in the end by draping all these differences in misleadingly similar colours. As Lawson has ably pointed out, we have integrated frustration as Freud imagined it into the general psychology of behaviour, but in doing so we have lost the beautiful simplicity of the accepted terms and embarked on the road to a more 'learned' and complex psychology.

2 Identification The same must be said of *identification*, the second point at which psychoanalysis relates to general psychology. We have already noted the place and importance of identification in the evolution of Freudian drives. There are two types of identification in Freudian theory (Bronfenbrenner). The first is responsible for the attachment the child forms for its mother, and it is particularly important in the first three stages (oral-respiratory-sensory, oral-incorporative, and anal-urethral-muscular). The second is completely different and explains how the child internalises his vengeful and awe-inspiring father. The first type of identification brings about a cordial fusion of the infant's self with the person of the mother, and thus explains how another person can become so integrated with the psychic organisation as to be indispensable. The second identification is tinged with hostility, and originates from the child's desire to replace his father in his mother's affections. This mechanism will enable the child eventually to satisfy the forbidden desire through another person, but he will also acquire the behavioural characteristics of the father with whom he identifies. He will internalise his father, particularly his father's rules of discipline, and create a kind of inner father who will become his conscience.

This complex Freudian idea has inspired a number of theories, such as those of Mowrer and of Parsons, and some experimental research. The idea has first been analysed into the following elements (Bronfenbrenner):

Identification as *behaviour:* the accent is on observable behaviour, and this goes on in the direction of direct or indirect imitation (imitation of the ideal: 'don't do as I do, do as I tell you').
Identification as *motivation:* the accent is on the intention to imitate.
Identification *process:* the accent is on the way in which the imitated behaviour is produced by the child in the course of his development.

On this basis, questionnaires have been constructed which are valuable instruments of research (Heilbrun 1965). But the greatest progress has been in the direction of objective enquiries. The work of Sears and his pupils is the most comprehensive.

For example, in their last report (1965) four-year-old children, boys and girls, were observed in well-defined situations in free play at their nursery school and in sessions with their mothers. Both parents also answered a wide-ranging questionnaire covering all aspects of the child's daily life and the parental attitudes. Finally, five major aspects of child behaviour were examined, each in some way referring to modifications of behaviour which Freud explained by the identification which is responsible for the development of the conscience: *dependence*, the way in which the child assumes the *adult role, aggression, sex typing and gender role*, and *conscience*. Each of these broad categories contains more specific types of behaviour. Dependence for example is analysed into five types of behaviour:

Negative attention-seeking (the child takes up an attitude of attack or opposition to gain attention, does the opposite of what he is told, etc.).

Reassurance-seeking (the child asks to be forgiven, requests permission when it is not necessary, seeks protection, consolation and guidance).

Positive attention-seeking (the child looks for praise, wants to participate in a group).

Touching and holding, non-aggressive clinging (the child holds on to another person, but not aggressively).

Being near (the child stays in the immediate proximity of an adult or a group of children).

If there were a global behaviour which could be called 'dependent behaviour', these various specific forms of behaviour would: (1) maintain high inter-correlations, or, at least, clearly follow each other with age, (2) have the same antecedents (in the behaviour of the mother, the father, or both parents). In fact there was a tendency for boys and girls to differ in this dimension, and the difference is significant for negative attention-seeking. But mostly the various types of behaviour show hardly any inter-correlation, which means that the same child can present some of them without the others; and furthermore, each type of behaviour has different determinants, not only from one type to another, but from one sex to the other.

Clearly these results are so impressive and the facts are so complex that the Freudian theory must be taken with caution: we must consider the determining factors, balance them against each other, define them in terms of the people involved, the parents as well as the child, and so proceed with the greatest possible care to explore the child's motivations.

Freud's original conceptions, in becoming integrated into the general psychology of childhood, have been modified, revised and reconstructed to such an extent that there seems to be nothing left of the original. This does not mean that the contribution of psychoanalysis has been forgotten. It has happened in the past that the originator of something did not realise the scope of his own discovery: the first modern men to cross the Atlantic believed themselves to be in China or India. The continent of drives discovered by Freud is still part of child psychology and further evidence of it will be seen in the course of this book.

5 Situations and relationships

In the phases studied this far, a certain aspect of behaviour was taken as a starting-point each time – now the level or function of intelligence, now the drives. However, as already noted, it was necessary in each case, within this limited field, to refer to determinants external to that field. Thus, intelligence cannot exist without reference to the drives and the drives of the individual stem to a great extent from the situations in which he is placed.

The third phase in child psychology both unifies and contradicts the previous phases. It does not partake of their bias. It borrows from the previous phases what appears important and rejects their limitations. In doing so, it does not merely collect the results, but lays deliberate emphasis on the child as a concrete totality.

One explanation for this new attitude is the sheer accumulation of facts, of isolated and specific items of knowledge. At the centre of each previous phase we have been able to place the name of a powerful personality or of a small group of individuals: Binet, Simon, Terman, Spearman, Thurstone, Piaget, Freud, Erikson. These early psychologists were, so to speak, individual craftsmen who worked single-mindedly developing their hypothesis, the ramifications and complexity of which would depend on the progress that had been made in individual research. Admittedly a group of workers collected round each of these men. But it always had a more or less authoritarian leader.

The striking characteristic of the new child psychology is that it is developed by research institutions rapidly becoming more important than single personalities. An institute for research into child welfare was established at the University of Iowa as early as 1917; similar institutes at the Universities of Minnesota, California and Columbia date respectively from 1925, 1925 and 1924. Counting only the most important, there are about twenty such institutes in the USA, without considering the research projects in progress at other universities, some of which carry over a number of years and involve several generations of workers. Similar laboratories are beginning to appear in Europe, and in all countries research is increasing, often thanks to workers trained in the major American or European centres who have returned to their own countries and founded new scientific establishments there.

The institutionalisation of research has led to increasing numbers of longitudinal studies. This is the name given to research carried out on the same subjects over a number of years. These studies have multiplied to the point where specialised bibliographies have to be compiled. like the one produced by Stone and Onque in 1959, which cites 297 studies up to 1955. Not all these studies are of equal importance, but there are at least ten, listed by Kagan in 1964, which may pass for major works and which have already added greatly to our knowledge and will do so yet more in future. The earliest studies concentrated particularly on somatic growth; later studies aimed at being as complete as possible, on the principle that it is easier to disregard certain information at a later stage than to start collecting it if it turns out to be necessary. The third and most recent type of longitudinal studies start out with a set of limited and precise hypotheses with which a 'strategic' sector of mental evolution is studied, such as the appearance of differences between individuals (Meili, at the University of Berne) or the origins of speech (the Brown groups). Because of this multiplication of research institutes, psychological publications on the child have proliferated to the point of necessitating annual 'reviews', in which a specialist in the field lists briefly all the articles and books which have appeared in a given period and tries to distinguish some major trends (thus a chapter on the child has figured in each issue of the *Annual Review of Psychology* since the first one in 1950). Provisional syntheses, like the recent books by the Hoffmans, are also published from time to time.

More important milestones, set at longer intervals, allow us to

94

33 Kurt Lewin (1890–1947).

see the principal trends in research more clearly. In the United States three dates – 1931, 1946 and 1963 – stand out in this way: each saw the appearance of a collective work presented as a 'manual' – that is to say, a collection of data accepted as valid by experts in the field. In the last chapter of the book which appeared in 1963, Bronfenbrenner makes a number of comparisons. In addition to what has been noted above, he calls attention to a stronger link between theory and experiment or observation. In the first phases of child psychology, theory often preceded observation in that it developed independently from a few observations originally linked and grouped around a certain theme. Since then the actual nature of theoretical construction has changed. It is now a matter of elaborating a limited, abstract model from which a few extremely limited forecasts can be made, which one attempts to verify by experiment. But this model, however limited, must remain within a more comprehensive framework defining what sort of variables should be used, what methods are considered valid, and what statistical tests will be required to establish a result.

All these trends are of undeniable importance. But behind the accumulation of detailed information which has resulted from institutional research, and behind the stricter awareness of the exigencies of scientific research, a new attitude may be discerned. The accent is differently placed; now it falls on the child's concrete situation. Most psychologists, in this respect, recognise Lewin as their 'godfather' in the previous generation.

Lewin was born in 1890 in a Baltic town, but was German by birth and nationality. He studied at Freiburg, where he met Wertheimer, the founder of the school of Gestalt, and then in Munich and Berlin. As a captain in the German army during the First World War, he applied the principles of the psychology of perception to the camouflage of his artillery. He was trained in the psychology of Associationism, then popular in Germany, and he later bridged the distance between this school and the new Gestalt psychology through the concept of drive: it is 'within' a drive that we can associate two elements easily, for instance two adjectives or an object and its name. After 1926, working in Berlin and then in the United States where he settled in 1933 and died in 1947, he concentrated his research on drives, doing experimental work on the major Freudian postulates, but creating theoretical models inspired by Gestalt psychology to explain them.

Lewin's central assertion has survived the 'topological' schemes which he derived, rather mischievously, from modern geometry. It is that: (a) behaviour must be derived from the totality of facts coexistent at the moment it occurs, and (b) these coexistent facts resemble a dynamic field in so far as the state of one part of the field depends on the state of all the other parts. With this assertion Lewin broke away from psychology oriented towards the future (for instance, the goals of action) or towards the past (associations or drives connected with the subject's history) in order to explore the impact of the present.

This approach involves considering not only the concrete information derived from objects in the field, but also the various milieux or environments which surround the author of the given behaviour. Even in the animal these concrete environments are both more complex and less varied than is generally thought. But in a human subject all of human nature is present in the least of his actions. To be more explicit, the human subject, and particularly the child with whom we are principally concerned, participates in several dynamic regions within the field. His behaviour is determined by the global society and its culture, which comprises both objects and attitudes; by the more immediate social environment or sub-culture, such as social class or socio-economic circumstances; by the limited global society of the family, with its diverse pressures resulting from the number of members of the family, the presence of both parents, their attitude to their children and to their home or both, and the number and sex of the older and the younger children. So one cannot completely understand any given behaviour without considering the many forces which have determined it quantitatively and qualitatively, and one will not understand the child's evolution, that is to say the chronological sequence of his behaviour, without taking these situations and with them the corresponding inner development into account.

Here it is worth mentioning an early attempt to show the totality of development in a concrete way: Olson's organismic age. The principle of this is quite straightforward: since each specific development partly obeys specific laws and also presents capricious variations in each child, it should be possible to obtain a better view of development by making a large number of simultaneous measurements in different fields. In this way one would obtain a sort of mean of development corresponding to the child's internal norm or personal law of growth. This law would be accelerated in some children and slower in others, and would make it possible to *individualise* our judgment of a child at a given stage, and to judge him, not partly in relation to an abstract reference population, but within the whole of his development and in relation to his own rhythm.

Olson proposed taking five somatic measurements (height, weight, force of grasp, skeletal maturity and number of second teeth) and five mental measurements (mental age, arithmetical age, reading age, academic age and social age), and calculating their mean. When the means were linked up they would produce a much more regular line than any of the constituents by themselves (figure 34).

The organismic age is interesting as it tries to relate all the dimensions of growth. It forces us away from a bias towards the family situation or the school, which usually oblige us to consider one or other of these developments and do not allow us to form a globally-based judgment. Nevertheless, this suggestion of Olson's has remained unproductive. Although it was made twenty-five years ago, it has given rise to virtually no research or attempts at application, and the tests to which it has been subjected, partial perhaps in both senses of the word, have not been positive enough to constitute much of a reproach to the indifference of clinicians.

The organismic age was in any case too simple a concept and, as such, belonged to earlier phases in child psychology. In practice more analytical approaches have been preferred. Here it is impossible to do more than touch on the various areas in which our knowledge has advanced. These areas are presented as large concentric circles, starting with the global society and proceeding to the family and the specific situation of the child among other children.

The child in society

We have mentioned the contribution of Freudian theory to cultural anthropology, and the way in which research on 'basic personality' is related to educational procedures. Data is continually being

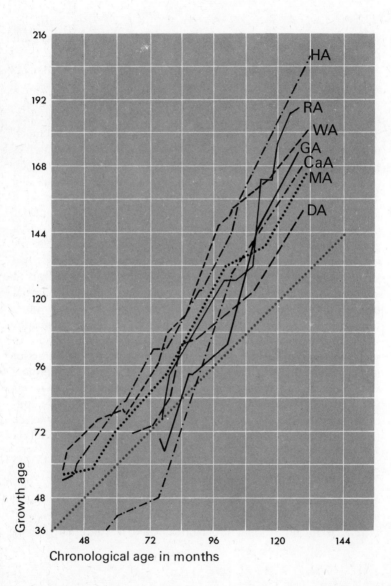

Growth age

Chronological age in months

34 A child's 'global' development is made up of a large number of partial developments — height (expressed here in height-age, HA), weight (WA), calcification of the bones (CaA), strength of grasp (GA), reading (RA) and intellectual performances (mental age, MA). These partial developments define the *organismic age* (Olson), which is more stable than any of its constituents alone. The diagram shows the growth of a girl who was studied over a number of years, and whose development is in advance of the mean of her group (development age, DA). By taking five somatic and five mental measurements at intervals (horizontal axis), Olson calculates the organismic age, which allows the quality of an individual's growth to be assessed.

accumulated on this theme. However, quantity is not always accompanied by precision. In future there will be a need for strict verification of hypotheses, which will be better formulated and limited to verifiable aspects of behaviour.

A promising line of research has been opened up by Barry, Child and Bacon, who explored certain aspects of material culture in some hundred primitive societies. They classified these societies according to whether they stored food supplies, and examined the relationship between this economic trait and educational practices. They found that a culture tends to lay stress on obedience and responsibility if it habitually stores supplies of food, and if it does not, its education lays stress on individual accomplishment, self-confidence and autonomy. If educational practices are reduced to a single dimension (*docility* versus *self-assertion*) an astonishingly high correlation of 0·93 is obtained, which practically allows one to predict educational attitudes from economic customs.

Working along the same lines, this group also studied the different treatment boys and girls receive in the course of their education. At first, in what we shall call early childhood, most cultures make very little distinction. But in later childhood a distinction emerges which is usually directly related to the differentiation between adult sexual roles: the boys are pushed towards self-assertion and action, while the girls are steered towards obedience, responsibility and maternally protective activities. However, the difference between educational practices for each sex varies from culture to culture. The difference is greatest in societies where the economy demands considerable physical effort, and in societies characterised by large family groups where there is a high degree of cooperation between all the members.

Studies of this kind emphasise the importance of the *material* environment in which the children grow up. It has been shown (by Roy) that the attitude of parents towards the aggression displayed by their children varies according to the number of rooms in the house. The same sort of differences appear in relation to sanitary installations and the safety of the immediate neighbourhood.

The child within a social class

However delicate a matter the definition of social class may be, modern society is so diversified that we cannot dispense with an intermediate unit between society, with its own structures and cultural aims, and the small family. It has been justly remarked that the individual is never familiar with the whole of his own culture, and that probably no one is capable of expressing this culture adequately in his behaviour. In practice everyone occupies a certain place in society, within a sub-group which usually has quite a clear hierarchy and on a certain rung of which he settles. The individual is therefore brought up by his parents in a way appropriate to the sub-culture and with an eye to the fairly circumscribed place he will take in society. These differences of social position and environment are, admittedly, disappearing in the many industrial societies which have grown up within the past thirty years. But to an enormous extent they continue.

It is not easy, however, to decide how these social requirements influence the child's development and education. The material culture has just been mentioned. This is certainly at the origin of the most striking differences between children in the same society. But there is also the question of different family atmospheres, as we shall see later. Too much importance has sometimes been attached to the details; the factors that distinguish most between social classes seem to be the general atmosphere, the aspirations of the parents, and the openness to scientific progress. Most of the relevant research work, which is somewhat imprecise, is American, and American social milieux unfortunately have particular characteristics which render comparisons with corresponding European milieux rather meaningless. In different countries, with different national traditions, there will inevitably be differences between corresponding social classes, and this is particularly true of the working class, who seem to differ more among themselves than the leisured classes, who have similar educational traditions which bridge the barriers between them.

An interesting hypothesis put forward by Miller and Swanson lends a certain subtlety to the simple idea of social class differences. They make the observation that someone engaged in a certain kind of enterprise has attitudes to work which will influence his attitudes to education and the ambitions he has for his children. The last century was an era of small enterprises created by one man, pushed forward by his own efforts and developed by constant initiative. The division of labour was minimal, the risk was considerable, the accent was on competition: the other person involved was a rival or a subordinate, and rarely a partner with whom it was possible to have a warm man-to-man relationship.

Within such a structure, parents had to accelerate their children's education. They urged them towards autonomy and control of their own lives, and they were eager for results. They tended thus to create opportunities for the children to assert themselves, particularly in face of the inanimate world or of society. They cultivated the taste for physical danger and strenuous competition.

Modern twentieth-century industry, in contrast, creates very large enterprises which are built on a series of levels of command and obedience. The emphasis passes from strenuous competition to promotion by merit and by seniority. This bureaucratic structure breeds new attitudes to education, compounded of patience, tolerance and good nature. Perhaps, too, the father of the family is more disposed to enjoy himself with his young children when he finds himself spending his working day in the grip of a huge in-human machine.

It is an attractive hypothesis. A limited attempt has been made to test it. The results are not conclusive, although they tend in the direction predicted.

The child in the family

1 The influence of the number of members of the family It was noted earlier that the modern family is usually limited to the parents and their young children. The number of people who participate in the everyday affairs of the small urban family is also usually restricted. These reductions have two important implications for the educa-tion of the child: on the one hand they limit the number of possible human interactions, on the other they impoverish the number of different roles.

Starting with the first point, we must remember that the number of relationships increases much more than proportionately in progressing from a pair to a group of three, four or five people. Between two people, **A** and **B,** the two parents for example, there are two relationships (that of **A** to **B** and that of **B** to **A**). If a child is introduced, there are now six relationships between three people: **A** to **B, B** to **A, A** to **a, B** to **a,** and their converse (**a** to **A** and **a** to **B**),

35 Rapid multiplication of human relationships when a group expands. Between two adults (A and B, husband and wife for example), there are two human relationships – that of A to B and vice-versa. When a child (a) arrives, the number of relationships increases disproportionately ; the previous relationships continue, but are augmented by the child's relationships with its parents. The picture may be complicated still further by introducing alliances (A+B towards a, A+a towards B – the child in league with his father against his mother, and B + a towards A – the child and the mother joining forces against the father). When the number of people in the group passes five, the relationships become extremely complex and their number increases very rapidly.

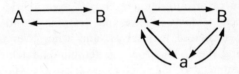

and there are even more (**AB** to **a,** or **BA** to **a**) which will not necessarily be identical if the two parents do not have the same educational attitude. The progression is extremely rapid. With two children various sub-groupings appear, showing lasting or short-lived alliances, complicities and rejections or exclusions which recreate earlier structures (before the birth of the second child). The systematic exploration of these different family situations is only in its early stages. A sociologist, Parsons, has founded a series of hypotheses on the differentiation of roles within the family unit. He applies Bales's observations on the general distribution of roles among groups studied in successive sessions – see figure 36. Two divisions emerge: one horizontal, which represents authority, the other vertical, which represents two opposing aspects of the directive role. It is unnecessary to dwell on the levels of subordination implied in the horizontal dimension; they are evident in all aspects of life in industrial society, and supremely important within the family. It is the vertical division that is new. It separates two different functions, both of which belong to a position of authority, but between which there is inevitably a certain tension. On one side there is the *instrumental* role: by this is meant a pattern of behaviour which ensures the attainment of the collective goal of a group. In Western civilisation this role is nearly always assumed by the man, who adheres closely to tangible things external to the group; the two occupations which best express this, the engineer and the soldier, are both explicitly masculine occupations. On the other side is the *expressive* role: this is less a matter of a fixed behaviour pattern than of an attraction exercised over inferiors which encourages them to love, admire and draw nearer to a person in whom they recognise themselves, and who gives assurance of understanding them. This role has feminine characteristics, even when it is assumed by men, whether in society as a whole (the priest) or in exclusively masculine groups (a club secretary, for example, or the sergeant-major who – in the Swiss army, at least – is responsible for domestic duties). Within the family it is usually assumed by the mother, while the instrumental role is in principle the father's. These distinctions, which appear very quickly in the life of a community, command different attitudes. The 'instrumental' superior is respected, his knowledge and intellectual powers are acknowledged, but he is not loved; the 'expressive' superior inspires devotion but is not the first to be consulted on a difficult matter, at least not as long as there is still hope. Here we see the origin of the ambivalence which Freud noted towards the parents: respect suffused with hostility for the father, and love, slightly condescending, for the mother.

These main divisions engender sub-divisions, such as the distinction within the instrumental role between the role of the technical expert and the executive role in the strict sense ('the man who knows how to do it' and 'the man who sees it gets done') or, on the other side of the principal axis, the distinction between the cultural and the religious role. Similarly, on a lower level, there are different shades of subordination; on the instrumental side the tension between the man who performs perfectly one particular act or skill, and the man who acts of his own free will, and so on.

These hypotheses emerged from sociological or psychosociological research, and refer to what occurs in groups which are more or less accidentally formed. They were retrospectively acknowledged to apply to the naturally-formed family group, and they are also relevant to a series of observations which have been made on the different influences of the father and mother on their children. M. M. Johnson notes that the father's instrumental role is more obviously typical of the man than the mother's expressive role is of the woman. All things considered, the mother is also instrumental to some extent, at least in one fairly comprehensive field – the daily life of the child. She guarantees his daily routine of meals, toilet, play and rest, and in suburban homes the father's prolonged absence reinforces this instrumental aspect of her activities. She is also less obviously a 'sexual' being than the father, and to some extent lacks salient characteristics which make identification and active imitation easy. This explains why boys who can identify with their father acquire more virile characteristics and are finally better adapted to their masculine role than boys who cannot (when for example the father is away for very long periods on military or naval service). On the other hand, there does not seem to be any relationship in girls between identification with the mother and adaptation to the feminine role. There is considerable evidence today that boys and girls react differently to parental intervention, and that boys are in general more sensitive to any disturbance of the 'normal' – i.e. socially acceptable – situation.

These pointers explain the importance of the number of people in the family circle. The roles are not so distinguishable when they cannot be incarnated in different actors. As the number of children

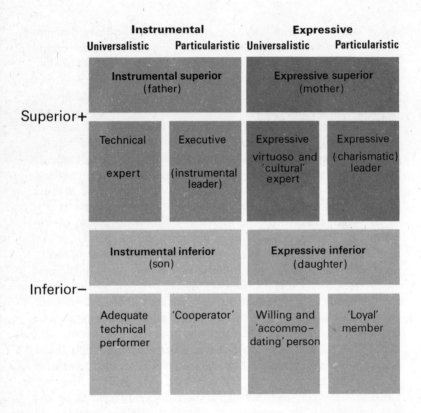

36 Parsons' schema emphasises the complexity of relationships within the family and, generally speaking, in the educational situation. There is first a major horizontal division of the groups into superiors (top) and inferiors (bottom). However, the 'superiors' are divided vertically into those who help the group to attain its collective goal ('instrumental' superiors) and those who polarise the emotion and loyalty of the group ('expressive' superiors). The instrumental role in turn has two aspects : the technical role (the person who knows how to do something) and the executive role (the person who gets it done). Similarly, the expressive role comprises the aspect of the virtuoso, who expresses perfectly the values of the group, and that of the priest, who promises salvation (the charismatic leader). Corresponding aspects are found in the inferior sector. In a large enough family, each of these roles will tend to be assumed by a different person.

increases, slight differences in their way of life become evident, largely because of the general pressure towards differentiation of actors in a constantly interacting group. Bossard was particularly interested in this phenomenon. He applied ethnological methods to families in his own environment, and counted the roles he observed in a study of sixty-four large American families. He discerned eight different roles played by the child:

1 The responsible child who can be counted on, rather domineering and imperious towards the others, frequently the oldest of the family
2 The sociable, lovable child, often the second
3 The 'social butterfly', all superficial politeness
4 The studious child
5 The solitary child
6 The irresponsible child
7 The sickly child
8 The spoilt child, often the youngest

There are naturally various reasons why each member of the family group assumes one role rather than another, and sometimes the choice is quite involuntary, as is the case with a long series of

Parent Behaviour Profile 2.2

Situation Home Visit
----

37 This working document embodies a family profile drawn up with the aid of the Fels Institute scales. Sigma (mean index) scores are indicated by dots on a grid which covers the extremes of each variable. The child, Theodore Stone, is six years and ten months old. As may be seen, the home is centred round the child, who is approved, accepted, surrounded with affection and perhaps too much helped and petted. This takes place within a rather authoritarian framework, without real understanding or much consequence; it is in other words a somewhat maladjusted and over-emotional family.

No.	Variable
1·91	Child-centredness of home:
5·2	Approval:
7·2	Acceptance:
8·3	Affectionateness:
8·4	Rapport:
2·12	Intensity of contact:
4·1	Babying:
4·2	Protectiveness:
7·1	Solicitousness:
3·21	Quantity of suggestion:
5·1	Readiness of criticism:
1·2	Activeness:
1·7	Coordination:
3·14	Justification of policy:
3·15	Democracy of policy:
3·3	Accelerational attempt:
6·1	Readiness of explanation:
8·1	Understanding
3·11	Restrictiveness of regulation:
3·22	Coerciveness of suggestion:
3·16	Clarity of policy:
3·12	Readiness of enforcement:
1·1	Adjustment:
1·5	Discord:
3·17	Effectiveness of policy:
3·18	Disciplinary friction:
1·6a	Sociability of family:
2·11	Duration of contact:
3·13	Severity of penalties:
8·2	Emotionality to child:

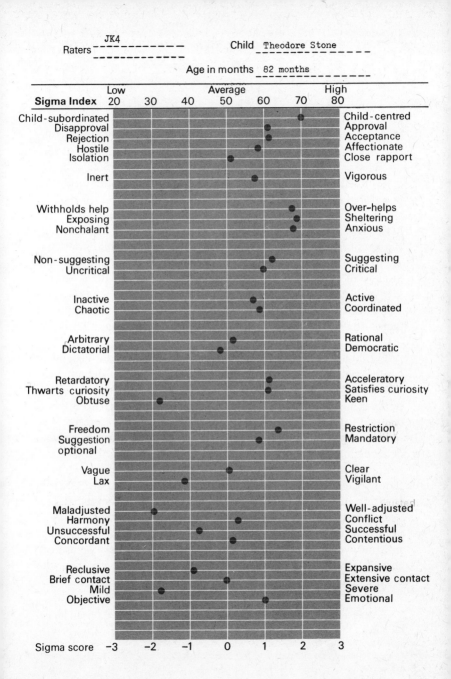

Raters ___JK4_____

Child ___Theodore Stone_____

Age in months ___82 months_____

Sigma Index	Low 20	30	40	Average 50	60	High 70	80	
Child-subordinated						●		Child-centred
Disapproval					●			Approval
Rejection					●			Acceptance
Hostile					●			Affectionate
Isolation				●				Close rapport
Inert					●			Vigorous
Withholds help						●		Over-helps
Exposing						●		Sheltering
Nonchalant						●		Anxious
Non-suggesting					●			Suggesting
Uncritical					●			Critical
Inactive					●			Active
Chaotic					●			Coordinated
Arbitrary				●				Rational
Dictatorial				●				Democratic
Retardatory					●			Acceleratory
Thwarts curiosity					●			Satisfies curiosity
Obtuse		●						Keen
Freedom					●			Restriction
Suggestion optional					●			Mandatory
Vague				●				Clear
Lax			●					Vigilant
Maladjusted		●						Well-adjusted
Harmony				●				Conflict
Unsuccessful			●					Successful
Concordant				●				Contentious
Reclusive			●					Expansive
Brief contact				●				Extensive contact
Mild		●						Severe
Objective					●			Emotional

Sigma score	-3	-2	-1	0	1	2	3

illnesses which channel a particular child into the role of the sickly one. Sociological determinants cannot explain everything, but they do have a certain importance as a network of practical truths determined by underlying social structures all too often neglected or ignored by pure psychologists.

2 Educational attitudes After the quantitative, the qualitative: the *content* of family life is much more important to the child's development than the simple framework within which he grows up. Studies in this field, initially inspired by research of a psychoanalytical type, have multiplied to the point where they now form an almost impenetrable jungle. However, through the techniques of factor analysis one can gain a high enough vantage point to see the main pathways.

The first rather unsystematic studies after the brilliant insights of psychoanalysis concerned the familial antecedents of delinquency. These marked the years 1910 to 1930. However, some time had to be spent in extricating work from the distorted comparisons which resulted from the use of a selected group instead of a representative series. It was therefore necessary to define the variables before determining their effect. From the 1930s onwards, lengthy longitudinal studies were set up to obtain factual information about the family background of the subjects being studied. The Fels Research Institute (USA) was particularly active in these attempts. It proposed very early to make an inventory of aspects of parental influence on children, approaching the subject without any preconceived ideas, but waiting to be guided by the facts themselves. In this way they obtained thirty scales, which they grouped into eight chapters (figure 37).

1 There is a general aspect which concerns the 'atmosphere' of the home, its human environment, its degree of tension, the extent of its intercourse with the outside world, the degree of structure in the family's daily business and the child's place in this unit.

2 The duration and intensity of the child's contacts with his mother are then assessed. This aspect directly reflects the particular circumstances of the American family, where particularly in the early years, the mother is usually in charge of the children's education, which is not the case in Europe. An English psychologist has recently found it necessary to plead on the father's behalf and criticise the 'mother-centred' character of American studies, showing that the absent parent is much more important than has been realised. French psychologists, adapting the Fels scales for French use, have been struck by the bias they reveal.

3 There are eleven scales for assessing the various kinds of control and influence exercised by the parents. Are the disciplinary rules restrictive or permissive? Are they applied strictly, being invoked at the smallest infringement, or fairly loosely? Are the punishments severe, and are they justified in the child's eyes by his own participation in promulgating the rules that are applied to him? Are they effective enough to make an impression on his behaviour? Are they frequent or rare? Does the parent work by suggestions, does he constantly intervene or hardly ever, and are his suggestions taken by the child as orders or just as advice? Does the family discipline try to accelerate the child's development, or is he deliberately left to grow at his own rate?

4 The fourth dimension combines two scales for evaluating the tendency of parents to over-protect their child.

5 The fifth attempts to measure the criticism levelled at the child (frequent or rare, oriented towards censure or praise).

6 This evaluates the parents' tendency to satisfy, or fail to satisfy, the children's intellectual curiosity.

7 The next dimension evaluates the warmth of the affective ties between the child and his parents.

8 Finally there is a grouping of four scales which evaluate the understanding shown by the parents, the emotional content of their reactions to childish behaviour, their manifestations of anxiety, and the degree of conjugal affection which ties them together independently of their relationships with the child.

These attempts at rigorous assessment are of great importance, and have enabled us to refine our techniques. They were made before the development of computers made the widespread use of statistical analysis possible. When the scales were first applied a number of principal dimensions were established. Three of these were retained; this produced by combination twenty-seven theoretically possible 'family atmospheres' (taking three degrees within each dimension: extreme positive, mean and extreme negative), but only seven of these were sufficiently represented in practice to justify relating them to their effects on the child's behaviour. Already at this level of analysis Baldwin, Kalhorn and Breese were able to show that the family environment exercised strong influence from the earliest moment when child development could be measured – that is to say, at the nursery school stage. 'Democratic' homes encourage the display of intelligence (the children's IQ tends to increase), and inspire originality and flights of imagination. 'Rejecting' families obstruct the child, who shows little originality or tenacity.

This research was still of the 'craftsman's' type, although it had already gone a long way in its analysis. Very shortly, however, methods of rapid calculation enabled it to go further still, and a number of factorial analyses of parental behaviour are now available. One of the first ones was Schaefer's 'circumplex'. This – to simplify its complexities – once again provided a way of analysing the data of the Berkeley longitudinal study (conducted principally by Nancy Bayley) – figure 38. The various parental attitudes were situated along two principal axes – love/hostility on the vertical axis, domination/autonomy on the horizontal. W.C. Becker has recently reviewed these studies and carried out more factor analyses with various methods. He believes it necessary to subdivide the horizontal dimension into two independent dimensions, one representing an imposed restriction of movements which

38 Schaefer's circumplex, obtained by the crossing of two principal axes, one opposing love and hostility, the other domination (of the parent) and autonomy (of the child). Between the extreme cardinal points various shades may be distinguished to describe actual families.

113

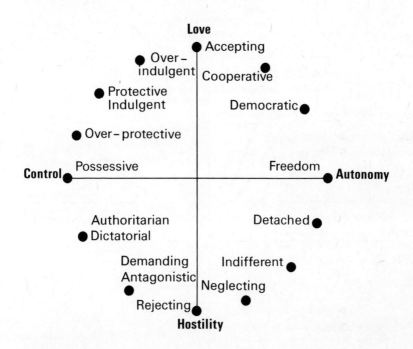

opposes permissiveness, the other representing the parent's emotional involvement in everything which concerns the child, ranging from anxious involvement to calm detachment. The dimensions then form a sphere (figure 39), inside which, by now familiar methods, the family atmosphere of most modern homes can be plotted.

The past mingles constantly with the present, here as elsewhere. A pilot study on the educational atmosphere of thirty families in a small rural community near Neuchâtel, which was on the verge of industrialisation, showed that the peasant family preserves a

39 Becker's sphere, defining family atmosphere in which a child grows up. Three axes cross at right angles ; the first two (restrictiveness-permissiveness, warmth-hostility) are familiar. The third (red) axis, which runs from back to front of the diagram, is detachment-anxiety. Any actual family may therefore be anywhere in this three-dimensional space ; situations to be visualised as being at the back of the diagram are shown with a dotted line.

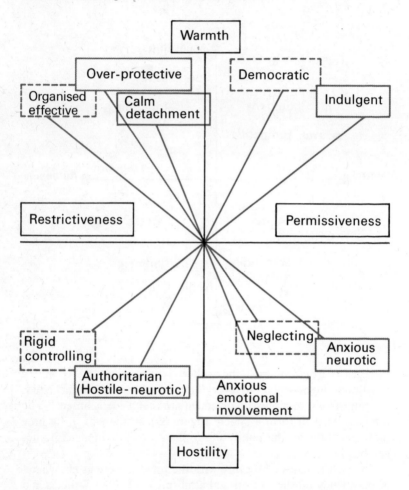

strongly-delineated structure. In most countries (including the USA) it comes within the 'authoritarian family' group. But on further analysis it becomes clear that the 'head of the house' is nature, the sun, the season, and the labour they impose. The father of the family merely formulates these into practical necessities. He does not exercise any arbitrary authority; he simply 'rules' the household as he rules his livestock. When this peasant family changes its way of life, for instance by augmenting its resources by means other than agriculture and thus entering on the cycle of industry, or by breaking away altogether from the daily agricultural routine, it retains its old educational practices. But they are no longer supported by the natural rhythm which had legitimised the father's authority. They take on an arbitrary colouring because they are now related to the father's or the parents' own will. Many working-class families, and not only families where the father runs his own business, come into this category. Before the family can become democratic, it needs to have lived for several generations in the town and to have improved its standard of living. Often it remains in the grip of peasant 'ideologies' after it has ceased to live by agriculture, and retains an authoritarian structure even in a democratic country.

The 'style' of a family cannot be determined solely by its educational methods. One must also consider the consistency, or lack of it, shown by the parents in exercising discipline, the relationship between the parents, the sex of the more dominant parent and the sex of the child. Each constellation is therefore specific, and has specific effects. From this group of determinants one must try to understand how the child develops. In this respect the aim of research is to define the questions more precisely. Research does not now ask what is the effect of a warm, democratic family atmosphere, but how this atmosphere facilitates originality, aggression, the internalisation of moral norms and the attainment of adult behaviour. We are not yet at the stage of being able to integrate all the information provided by longitudinal studies and systematic observation into a unified view, and in any case this is perhaps impossible, given the extreme complexity of human affairs in modern society.

3 Sibling rank and characteristics The same must be said for the other aspects of the family environment. For a time it was hoped that certain trends could be related to the child's position in the family – a constellation of chances and risks which would be specific for the oldest child, the youngest, and the second child. In earlier societies this position had some importance. The eldest son inherited the property, the youngest often became a soldier. The second son, according to the Hindu proverb, was 'the child of God'. It would seem natural to expect that, in the small modern urban family, the positions would emerge even more clearly. Persistent attempts have therefore been made to determine their effect. Unfortunately this research has often suffered from a lack of stringent criteria. As it produced conflicting results a more critical approach was made, and it became apparent that the first-born of a series of brothers and sisters was being confused with the only child, who certainly held the same sibling rank, but whose circumstances were completely different.

There is a group working at present in this field (Koch), and one hopes they will be able to unravel this tangled skein of family patterns. They have already discovered certain rules in American families, for instance the fact that the second child, if it is a girl and follows a male first-born, tends to acquire more masculine ('tomboyish') characteristics than if it follows a sister. These influences are particularly strong when there is only a short interval between the births. With an interval of two to four years the tension seems to increase. A boy who has several older sisters seems more dependent in his relationships with other people and less ready to assert himself, as if he had too many maternal models who reinforced his submissiveness and discouraged his aggression.

The study is so far only in the early stages of the child's development, and the effect of these circumstances on the pre-adolescent child and the young man or woman is not yet known.

The child with his peers and his school class

Some progress has been made, on the other hand, in measuring the social atmosphere. Complex studies have been carried out on small groups. However, little is known in detail about the formative effect of the atmosphere. On the strength of observations made on animals, especially mice, it is believed that placing an aggressive child in a group of other aggressive children will make him quieter, and conversely, that placing an over-submissive child in a non-aggressive group will stimulate aggression in him. Many studies have been made on the stability of childhood friendships (figure 40), the qualities which make for popularity at given ages, the traits which isolate a child from his playmates, and the influence of different styles of authority. But these influences are revealed only at a comparatively late stage in development, when the main personality characteristics are already discernible. The same may be said for the school atmosphere. This, even in a well-conducted class, is clearly more authoritarian than democratic, and certainly has a temporary effect on children's behaviour. Whether it also has a formative effect on the personality which is felt many years later we cannot yet say. New teaching techniques which modify the human elements of schooling are being introduced, and some useful comparisons will be possible between different types of interaction among schoolchildren, and a clearer definition of the educational role of the school.

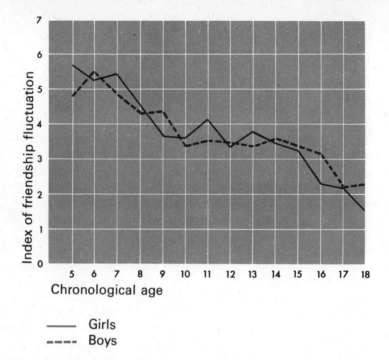

Girls

---- Boys

This chapter has shown the main lines of research and the progress that has been made. Everything that concerns the child and his development is extraordinarily complex. The number of variables is increasing rapidly. Thus in one of his studies Sears divides parental intervention into six hundred different headings, and relates each one of them to a form of behaviour observed in the child. We have come a long way since the rash generalisations of the last generation of scientists, when it was thought possible to account for the important aspects of adult personality by one or two easily-located determinants. But we are moving towards a profounder and more precise concrete psychology, which will be guiding the parents of the next century.

For educational practices are changing, although slowly. It is perfectly natural for parents to want to give their children 'what was good for them'. One is warned against this temptation in the Talmud. It entails the risk of preparing the adults of tomorrow for

40 Instability of friendship is the rule at the beginning 119
of school life. Boys and girls change their partners freely
in work and play. Between ten and fourteen years friendly
relations become somewhat more stable, and the stability
is further confirmed at adolescence. Fidelity is now
the rule, although rather more so among girls than boys.

the world of yesterday. The impact of the change which has over-taken our societies can be seen, for example, in the changing advice given to parents in popular books or the columns of national papers. These documents, together with school textbooks, have been studied many times. The advice they give starts with the first days of life. A young mother of today would be extremely surprised if anyone approached her about the subject which was her great-grandmother's principal concern: getting a good wet-nurse for her newborn baby. There is advice on this subject dating from the sixteenth century, but as late as 1879 a practitioner, Caldwell, was insisting that the chosen nurse should have a good hereditary dis-position, recommending mothers to avoid blondes and redheads because they were too passionate, and to choose brunettes who, since their milk was less troubled by emotion, had the advantage of calming the excitement of precocious babies. Among 644 articles which appeared on the feeding of babies between 1890 and 1948, the vast majority recommended breast-feeding, but the reasons put forward move from the medical to the psychological or emotional plane. One author writes of a 'sentimental' phase which exalts the mother's role, a rigid phase oriented towards early discipline of the child, with the accent on making him achieve self-control quickly, and a phase where the accent passes to the child's self-regulation and happy understanding. It is only in recent publications that one finds assurances that artificial feeding of the newborn is not necessarily injurious, or that parents are advised to be patient and not rush the child's toilet-training. The latest edition of the popular American booklet *Infant Care* is distinguished from its predecessors by the absence of dogmatism on the possible effects of particular educational practices, and by its revelation of the immense variety of the infant's responses to the actions of adults towards him. The accent passes completely from the particular to the general; emphasis is placed on the importance of a stable emotional bond which seems to count for more than the minutiae of maternal care.

This leads us naturally to ask in the following chapter what childhood means in the long term and how our educational practices should be geared to accord with this meaning.

6 What is normality ?

It is difficult not to wonder what childhood 'means', and equally difficult to answer the question. The psychologist, as a scientist, avoids the question of value. In his eyes all behaviour has the same interest, in that it requires explanation and refers to general models or theories. But this suspension of value-judgments cannot last indefinitely. For one thing, it is to psychology that one turns to understand, or in other words to rectify, anomalies of development. For another, parents and educationalists need psychology to guide their handling of children (this, as we have seen, is one of the reasons for the rapid growth of modern child psychology). Thus clinicians and educationalists, implicitly or explicitly, pose the problem of finding a norm of development. The pure scientist may repudiate the insistence of his practical colleagues, and may be disturbed to find himself dragged into the realm of values from which, historically speaking, he has taken such pains to dissociate himself; but he would be wiser to admit the existence of the problem instead of dwelling on its ambiguities.

How then shall we define childhood, and what is its place in life as a whole? What exactly is its function? We shall begin by using a biological approach to these difficult questions.

Human and animal childhood

At first glance, human childhood does not seem harder of definition than animal childhood: a period of life occupied mainly by growth and development towards adulthood. But modern biologists such as Portmann warn us against over-facile analogies. We are now emerging from the intellectual climate inaugurated by Darwin in the last century when it was particularly important to stress whatever linked man with the animals and to emphasise the solidarity between neighbouring species. After centuries in which man had tried to set himself apart from the rest of creation, in a privileged position guaranteed by a special divine plan, it was doubtless then necessary to attack this vanity by the idea of the evolution of all species and thus reaffirm man's relationship with all the other forms of life on Earth. Now, by a swing of the pendulum familiar in the history of ideas, we are no longer so anxious to animalise mankind. This does not mean questioning what has been established. We know that our physical structure resembles that of other species, that our physiological functioning is very similar, and that certain of our hormones are identical. But we are more aware of the differences, and it may be necessary at this stage to 'rehumanise' man, stressing the things that distinguish him from the nearest related species – not by his ability to use tools or by his strength, where the difference is all too apparent, but in the very realm where we would expect to find our animal nature: in biological structures.

From a mass of facts compiled over twenty years by Portmann, we will select a few which are generally overlooked.

1 Childhood in animals is *short*, even in relation to the life-span. The tiger, which lives to twenty years, reaches its adult height at eighteen months. The sperm whale is 7 metres long at birth and 14 metres long at seven months, and scarcely grows at all after the second year (the male grows on average to 22·6 metres and the female to 23·7 metres).

Coming nearer to the human race, in the anthropoids, who live to about thirty, the gorilla stops growing at about six, the chimpanzee at eleven to twelve, and the orang at twelve to thirteen. Sexual maturation occurs shortly before growth finishes. In man, growth continues until about nineteen, although sexual maturity is achieved at about fifteen. What is more, this maturity is heralded by a new spurt of growth, to which there is no equivalent in related species.

Human childhood therefore takes up a quite considerable

proportion of the life-span. Biologically it is remarkable for its unusual length.

2 The newborn of species related to man are already very close to adult proportions; the baby chimpanzee bears much more resemblance to the adult chimpanzee than the human newborn does to the human adult. A scale based on eleven measurements has been worked out for calculating the difference between the fifteen-week-old foetus (which is still very similar in all related species) and the adult form. The difference is 6·7 in the orang, 7·7 in the gibbon, 7·9 in the chimpanzee, 9·8 in the gorilla, and 23·4 in the human being. This means that between the human foetus and the adult a complete recasting of proportions takes place. Human childhood, in comparison with that of animals, seems to be *slowed down:* our animal relatives reach their final dimensions more quickly; we arrive later and more slowly.

3 The human race seems to contradict something like a biological law which determines the degree of independence the newborn possesses at birth. In mammals with a simple nervous system (as in numerous insectivores) a number of well-defined associated characteristics are found: a short gestation (20–30 days), a large number of young per litter (5–22), and a completely helpless newborn, born with its eyes shut. On the other hand, as the nervous system becomes more complex the gestation becomes longer, the number of young decreases, but there is a higher 'level of achievement' at birth. The young are born with their eyes open, and can very soon perform actions which involve a considerable degree of organic autonomy. This is particularly true of the anthropoids. The length of gestation in the chimpanzee (about 253 days) and the orang (about 275) has been painstakingly calculated, although it has not been definitely established in the gorilla. However, it is almost as long as human gestation (average 266 days).

The number of young in the anthropoids is small: one or two to a litter, as with humans. But it is the autonomy of the young that is most striking. They are born with their eyes open, and from the first day of life are capable of a large variety of movements. They do not leave their mother, admittedly, but they cling to her with their own strength, by an instinctive reaction which guides their activity from the moment they are born. Chimpanzees are seen to stand upright at the age of one month. At six months the mother leaves the young to accustom them to independence.

The human newborn presents a curious mixture of traits. He is born with his eyes open, and there is usually only one child from a pregnancy. In this he resembles the anthropoids. But he is completely helpless, and even late in his first year he would certainly die if no one looked after him. In this he resembles the inferior mammals.

4 These paradoxical traits are clarified in Table 3, which shows the weight, and particularly the brain-weight, at birth. This table shows that the newborn of the three species of anthropoids shown are all about the same weight, in spite of the difference in height between their mothers, and that this weight is markedly lower than that of the human newborn (in man, almost all newborn weigh slightly over 3 kilograms, whatever the height of the mother). But it also shows that while the mean birthweight of man is double that of the anthropoids, the mean brain-weight is almost treble, and this is the principal reason for the growth we have discussed.

5 The helplessness of the human newborn seems to arise from the disproportion between his brain-weight and his bodily mass. To balance his bodily growth in terms of his cerebral growth he would need to continue growing for several months. In other words, as Portmann puts it, the human newborn is *physiologically premature*. He is 21 months old before he is as fully developed as the anthropoid is at birth. To put it yet another way, the whole of the first year (which roughly corresponds to the lactation cycle) represents

Table 3 Comparative biological data of man and anthropoids

	Gestation (days)	Weight at Birth (in grams)			Coefficient of growth
		Total weight	Brain weight	Adult brain	
Gorilla	?	1500–1800	ab. 130	430	3·3–3·6
Chimpanzee	253	1890	ditto	400	ditto
Orang	275	1500	ditto	400	ditto
Man	266	3200	360–385	1450	3·6–3·9

an extra-uterine gestation; this throws light on the essential characteristics of the first year, and particularly the infant's absolute dependence on his mother.

6 The increased physical mass of the brain is not simply a quantitative matter, in the sense that man has more neurones than his animal ancestors. It also corresponds to a higher degree of 'cerebralisation'. (This term refers to the more 'recent' parts of the brain, which are responsible for associations and integrated thought, in contrast to the cerebral masses which are phylogenetically 'older'.) This superiority was already apparent in the calculation of Dubois (1897), and can be seen still more clearly in those of the Zoological Institute of the University of Basle. The cerebral index in man is now given as 170·0, as against 49 for the chimpanzee and 34 for the macaque. The increase is accounted for by the most recently-developed parts of the brain, to the neglect of the older parts. These older parts contain the inherited knowledge which is expressed in what we call 'instinctive' behaviour. The newer areas mainly control fine adaptations to external and internal signals, and the higher aspects of social life.

Man, the animal without instincts

The heading to this section holds a statement of the greatest importance. We should pause to consider it for a moment. The real difference between animal and man does not lie in the outward form but in the behaviour, or type of behaviour, of which man is capable. Anglo-Saxon psychologists have tended to neglect this point because they have usually tried to explain behaviour by the principles of habit-formation, of which there are many examples on the animal level, particularly in the rat. In fact habit has relatively little scope in animal behaviour. It is more important to note what the animal cannot do or learn than what it will manage to do in the artificial conditions of a laboratory. In its natural state, the animal is adapted to its environment by a set of inherited behaviour-patterns which are released by arbitrary signals. These behaviour-patterns are mechanical in that, once triggered off by an appropriate sensory stimulus, they generally work through their entire sequence. Thus the foal does not have to learn how to trot; along with his hooves he inherits the ability to use them. If the experimenter artificially disturbs the 'natural' sequence (that is, the usual constellation of signals to which the animal is attuned by heredity), he will of course reveal the role individual experience plays in a stereotyped pattern of behaviour. But the fact that the animal belongs to a specific environment, which presents the signals it must react to in order to preserve its own life and assure the survival of its species, means that a species can be recognised as accurately by its behaviour as by its external form (its 'morphology').

There is no parallel to this in humans. Although, biologically, man constitutes a distinct species (if only judged by the richness of his development), he presents such different patterns of behaviour that they do not seem to belong to one and the same family. Admittedly the need for food and shelter, for self-defence and for reproduction are common to all cultures, but these cycles of activity are translated into vastly different behaviour in different peoples. Men differ as widely in what they eat, how they eat, and in what circumstances and what manner, as do animal species of different morphological structure.

Man therefore does not inherit a set of indispensable rules which prepare him for all normal situations in a predetermined environment. Nonetheless, he would die if he were not prepared for the dangers of his environment. He must therefore construct this indispensable repertoire of behaviour himself. This is precisely the function of childhood. Childhood may thus be defined as *the period during which the human being, through his own efforts and with the guidance of education, constructs a system of behaviour adapted to the normal circumstances of life.*

Man as the product of man

The last point is extremely important. The formation of habits occupies a strategic place in the human being. It begins with the first days of life. It modifies the inherited rudimentary schemes which the organism uses in its earliest adaptations – sucking, swallowing, sleep, evacuation. But above all it gives structure to the massive and undifferentiated activity of the newborn, by giving precise meaning to external events and refining the motor adaptation to the environment.

Hebb, working from a neurophysiological concept, suggested that two types of learning should be distinguished: primary habit-forming, which is structural and responsible in man for the 'construction of reality', and secondary habit-forming, which constructs a network of more voluntarily-acquired abilities on the basis of what has been acquired earlier. This would explain the importance of the first days of life, of the family environment, and of the basic personality which remains a permanent part of the adult and is responsible for the distinguishing features of different cultures. It does in any case explain the very slow maturation of human beings and the length of childhood. It seems in fact, as Hofstaetter suggests, that the maturation rate is in inverse proportion to the value of the cerebral index, although the complexity of the behaviour learnt depends directly upon this value.

If this is so, biology will not provide us with the inner norm of mental evolution. Biology shows us an organism deprived by its heredity of stereotyped forms of behaviour and having to acquire them through contact with the world, and in particular through the cultural environment. Man is the first product of his own civilisation. But the adult form which is attained through childhood is, historically speaking, only relative. There is no one way of being human; there are as many ways as there are different societies and different traditions.

Tensions from man's dual status

Does this mean there is no way of relating different cultures? The question is no longer an academic one, because technical progress has made the world a smaller place, and from now on we shall be in close contact with many different ways of life. Can I regard this stranger as a 'normal' person when he is of a different height and complexion from me, eats strange food in a different way from the way I eat, dresses oddly, has a strange manner of greeting, behaves towards his wife in a way I find incomprehensible and treats his children without respect for my own educational principles? Has he the right to be what he is? 'How could anyone possibly be Persian!'

In the past the problem was usually solved by fire and the sword. The stranger was the enemy: many languages use the same word for the stranger and the man who must be destroyed. Moreover, most societies describe their way of life by a term which implies that it is the only valid way of life. All strangers are animals with human faces, who can only make noises like 'ba ... ba ...' (barbarians), and can legitimately be enslaved. How do we know that they have souls like us? Even among the primitive inhabitants of New Caledonia, 'the man' (*Do Kamo*) is only 'the native'.

These feelings have not disappeared. They were behind the shocking mass murders of our own lifetime, and they will no doubt cause others. They create tension in large industrial countries – white against black, native against foreign workers. Even so, these feelings are now in conflict with other feelings, of gathering strength, which recognise that particular cultures must open out into a broader human culture, where the things that are common to all men will be affirmed.

Normal man in industrial civilisation

Industrial civilisation involves an 'actor', a certain type of man. He is difficult to define in a way that would be universally accepted. The question of what constitutes 'normality' is still being debated, recently with great vigour. The meaning of the word changes with the user of it. To the anthropologist, the normal man is the one whom his compatriots, in a given society and at a precise moment of time, accept as normal. This makes the concept of normality dependent on conformity to a social standard. The statistician tends to define normality by maximum frequency. For him, even lying is normal in that a great many people are not unduly worried by small distortions of the truth and quite easily adapt to making such distortions. By this definition, tax evasion is 'normal' in most countries. But as soon as one applies this statistical concept to traits which are desirable, such as intelligence, one sees its limitations: is it not less 'normal' to be capable of only a short term of schooling, as most people are, than to be able to carry on to the end of higher education? At this point the clinician intervenes: normality is not the usual pattern (for instance, almost everyone has some nervous habits), but the exemplar. This exemplar is manifested partly in social conformity (although no civilisation is perfect enough to be presented as the only possible one), but largely in a capacity for personal fulfilment. Modern man is haunted by this ideal and the inability to attain it involves varying degrees of psychic suffering (and often, when the psychic illness affects bodily function, varying degrees of physical illness as well).

Attempts have been made (by, among others, Saul, Mowrer, Cole, Duykaert and particularly Fromm) to define the conditions necessary to the realisation of this ideal by eight 'criteria' of normality. These criteria naturally constitute the aims of education and thus act as guiding ideas in the psychology of development. (They are the 'tasks' which the child must take on and resolve between infancy and maturity, which will be considered in detail in the second part of the book.)

1 Ideal normality means that the individual has achieved complete independence (the *individual* task). This process starts with the fertilisation of the ovum and the foetus is already a self-regulated organism with an independent circulation. A series of liberations then have to take place in order for the newborn, then the young child, and finally the adolescent to sever his close relationship with his parents and arrive at the stage of creating his own family. Independence therefore has to be first biological, then physical, then alimentary, then socio-psychological, before it can finally become emotional. Development may stop short at any one of these stages, and the individual will then become to some degree a 'parasite' – there are many adults who trail an invisible umbilical cord behind them. And when independence of the real parents has apparently been achieved, many still avoid complete independence by choosing symbolic parents to replace them.

2 Independence is without doubt the most obvious characteristic of maturity. To it, however, must be added the ability to create. The young child receives everything and gives nothing; he then reaches the stage of being able to reciprocate, and slowly moves towards the stage of fair exchange. Even the most exemplary adult cannot give all the time; he continues to receive. But he strikes a balance between what he takes and what he gives, and what he gives is an expression of himself. Giving integrates the adult in a community based on exchange, and in economic terms it takes the form of a man's profession or vocation. Industrial civilisation eloquently testifies to man's creative power. To participate in this creativity in one's own way, whatever it may be, is the fulfilment of individual development.

3 The subjective side of this creative ability, the capacity for relaxation and happiness, is also important. For the clinician the touchstone of normality is in this 'psychological tone'; he would not consider a man completely adult (or ideally normal) if he were serious at an inappropriate time and could never abandon himself to the pleasures of the moment. The capacity for happiness and human warmth represents a slow conquest of the feelings of inferiority, egoism and rivalry which plague childhood, and it also represents the control of an adult form of aggression, more often directed against things or situations than against people as such. It is accompanied by a certain sentiment towards oneself, the *jouissance loyale de son être*, which Montaigne saw as the outcome of the effort to become a person.

4 The exemplary adult has assimilated the norms of morality in such a way that he can adapt them flexibly to circumstances. He knows that extremes of right border on the extremes of injustice (*summum jus summa injuria*), and that there is a way of applying the letter of the law which reveals an inner inadequacy, but he also knows that there is a moral direction to all of our lives without which they would be a long desert. The application of morality is a particularly complex matter in our civilisation, where technological and social changes have upset the traditional sources of moral judgment, and it is one of the great debates of adolescence. But it is prepared at a very early stage by the assimilation and, later, the modification of the norms of the environment, both of which are necessary for the forming of a critical attitude. Through this ethical maturation the individual becomes able to communicate significantly with other people, to balance his rights and his obligations in the community and thus to participate in communal tasks.

5 Because of its importance, sexual evolution must be considered separately from moral evolution. The basis here is a certain disposition of the body and bodily movements; the affective side of this is, predominantly, the ability to give in taking and to take in giving, and the possibility of experiencing the cycles of pleasure, labour and rest in harmony with another person and in the greatest possible intimacy.

6 Although perfect maturity is not primarily a question of intelligence, it cannot be achieved without the ability to understand, at least in outline, the essentials of environment and time, concepts which allow us to orient ourselves in the world. In this sense maturity involves some degree of success in the task of learning, and demands a permanent effort on the part of the individual to inform and educate himself.

7 There is a certain flexibility in the adult's mastery of himself and of reality. The adult is 'master of himself and the universe'; he 'seeks self-mastery more than riches, and to change his desires more than the way of the world'. This does not mean that there is no guiding line; it is not always 'healthy' to be too adaptable when

the circumstances themselves are inhuman – too much flexibility is as harmful as too much rigidity. Nonetheless, the adult will bend without breaking under many hardships, and can distinguish between the inessentials, on which compromise is always possible, and the essentials, where to concede would destroy his reasons for living. This constant analysis is not merely a challenge to his intelligence: an understanding of reality is proof of the maturity of the heart.

8 Lastly the adult is aware to some extent of his own abilities and limitations; he lives with his eyes open. This means that he has achieved a certain attitude to the world around him, has clarified his relationship to 'what transcends him', to other people and to his own future, and in this way has created a certain philosophy or set of reasons for pursing his own particular way of life.

These eight points can be combined into one statement: the perfect adult is *responsible*. The term contains the word *response:* the adult responds to the stimulations of the environment, the needs of others and the demands of the moment. His response is personal in that it expresses him, but at the same time it links him to the community like an instrument in an orchestra. Perfect normality is the road towards a collective destiny, on which the future of man might one day be founded. However, this is not the place to discuss such a question. We shall confine ourselves to saying that childhood ends with the attaining of civic rights, after which the individual embarks on a new existence as an adult, participating in the human struggle to dominate nature and organise the civilised world.

If these are the goals of mental evolution in democratic industrial society, they should provide a criterion for educational methods. Good methods increase the individual's chances of reaching perfect maturity. Bad methods retard or hinder this maturation. It has been suggested that the adult's attitude to the child is either 'educative' or 'instructive'. The 'educator' never loses sight of the long-term objective and, at any given moment, will choose an educational measure which leads on to future learning. The 'instructor' responds to the immediate situation with immediately-effective measures, and deals with the particular problems of any given moment without thinking about the possible repercussions of his action. The 'educator' relates his demands to the child's capacities at this precise moment in his development. The 'instructor' commands or forbids in the abstract. Gesell gives an amusing example of this difference. A four-year-old child is sat down at table and has some difficulty in coordinating all his movements at the same time – what he has to do to bring a full spoon to his mouth, and what his feet and legs are doing almost uncontrollably under the table. This results in a series of kicks which the adult finds intolerable. The 'instructor' reprimands the child and perhaps even punishes him: he thinks the child is capable of self-control. The 'educator', who knows he is not, will have put a pair of slippers on the child in the first place, so that the kicks do not hurt.

A description of the 'normal' man (normal in our society at this time) does more than act as a guide to the educator. It also allows childhood to be seen as a succession of related tasks, the mastery of which brings the child to maturity. This idea forms the basis of the second part of the book, in which childhood will be surveyed in its principal stages.

7 The main divisions of childhood

So far we have dealt with the main problems of childhood, and with the way modern psychology has gathered together the knowledge which will be used by the educator. Childhood is a period of preparation which leads a being who is completely helpless at birth to a relatively integrated adulthood, an 'ideal' picture of which has been presented. However, this evolution has to be divided into chronological sections. Clearly a child does not become adult overnight, at least not in modern industrial society even if this is the case in more primitive communities. (The purpose of initiation ceremonies is to bring the adult out from the chrysalis of childhood.) Nor does the child mature on all levels at once.

For the growing child evolution is continuous. It is also continuous for his parents, who are too close to him to be able to see the changes until these are too striking to be ignored. This unbroken development is inwardly duplicated by a continuity of consciousness. It seems then that the essential characteristics of childhood can only be conveyed by an historical account.

Furthermore, there is no such thing as childhood, only children who express their own unique personalities from a very early age – from birth, in fact. Each child comes into the world in unique circumstances, endowed with an individual genetic make-up. He becomes part of a particular family situation and is influenced by surroundings and events which affect him alone. Even brothers and sisters structure the same family environment in different ways and thus cause it to be different in each case. Twins, even identical twins, have totally individual histories.

Yet for all this, these individual histories do present similarities, and the onlooker, and the individual himself when he succeeds in remembering, recognises certain culminating points which break childhood up into phases or periods. It is in any case necessary from a practical point of view to organise an historical account into successive chapters even if the divisions are arbitrary.

The scientific literature abounds with suggestions as to what divisions should be adopted, and this abundance is more of a hindrance than a help. If anything it shows that none of the schemes put forward has a totally objective basis. However, it also shows that childhood can be approached and organised from many different angles.

Divisions and timings of physical growth

The collective growth curve for weight (heavy line in figure 42) shows three clear-cut stages: the first from birth to the beginning of the third year, when physical growth is carried forward by the prenatal impetus; the second, which is linear, from the third to the tenth year, when growth is slower; and the third which represents the resumption of growth at adolescence and ends when adult stature is reached. This gives us the stages of infancy, childhood and adolescence – three major periods which involve different problems in the general equilibrium of the body and different problems in the child's behaviour.

Individual curves are often more irregular. They show the initial spurt of growth and the linear growth of the following years, but there is often a dip the sixth year. (Some authors have taken this to indicate a period of somatic 'crisis' but it is more likely to be a result of the way starting school affects a number of children.) The intensive growth in the tenth year is even more marked, and the start of adolescence more dramatic.

Height, muscles and bone structure, which follow the first growth curve, are of course only one part of the body. Other kinds of growth, which are less apparent, follow other laws. Neurological development, affecting the brain (broken lines in figure 42), shows rapid growth initially, but the growth does not slow down at the end of the second year as in the first curve. The initial spurt

42 There are two distinct periods in the growth of an organism, separated by birth. In the first period the various tissues grow at the same rate (or almost). In the second, five clearly-distinguished curves appear. The first represents the skeletal and muscular masses (heavy line). The brain and nervous system (broken solid line) grow rapidly until the age of six years, by which time they have achieved over ninety per cent of their ultimate size. Three other groups, which are mainly concerned with maturation, grow in unison. Childhood may be divided into stages according to when these various curves begin and end.

continues until the sixth year, when the neural mass has grown to nine-tenths of its eventual size. It then grows imperceptibly for the next fourteen years.

The maturation of the nervous tissue follows a unique course. All the neurones are formed by the fifth month of gestation and their subsequent development does not involve a multiplication of the cells but a physiological process of completion, particularly in the development of the myelin sheaths which isolate the nerve fibres and allow them to function properly. Sub-stages in the construction of the nervous system have been suggested, which divide the first months of life according to the functional predominance of certain parts of the brain over the rest of the nervous system. This would give an initial sub-cortical phase which would correspond to the lactation phase, and, roughly, to the 'extra-uterine growth' of the biologists. Seen in this light, the age of six constitutes a definite stage. It roughly corresponds to the age of school entry.

The other three curves seem to be coordinated. They concern the tissues which are directly involved in sexual maturation. The genital tract, strictly speaking, is static from birth to the age of ten or eleven. It then grows to its full extent within about eighteen months. The development of the adrenal glands follows much the same course, but is rather more accentuated, showing an initial

139

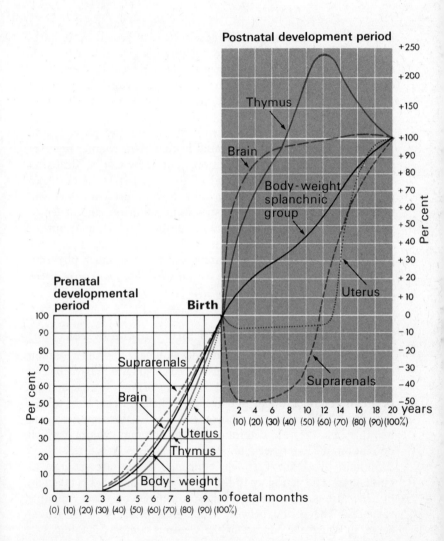

Postnatal development period

Thymus

Brain

Body-weight
splanchnic
group

Uterus

Suprarenals

+250
+200
+150
+100
+90
+80
+70
+60
+50
+40
+30
+20
+10
0
-10
-20
-30
-40
-50

Per cent

2 4 6 8 10 12 14 16 18 20 years
(10) (20) (30) (40) (50) (60) (70) (80) (90)(100%)

**Prenatal
developmental
period**

Birth

Suprarenals

Brain

Uterus

Thymus

Body- weight

100
90
80
70
60
50
40
30
20
10
0

Per cent

0 1 2 3 4 5 6 7 8 9 10 foetal months
(0) (10) (20) (30) (40) (50) (60) (70) (80) (90) (100%)

regression and a slightly earlier acceleration of growth, and finishing at the same time. The thymus, the physiological role of which is still uncertain, starts by growing at a considerable rate which slows down during adolescence. In combination these cause the turbulent physical growth associated with adolescence and genital maturation. The turning-point is eleven to twelve years.

Other glands follow other growth curves, and each physiological function has its own developmental history. This chapter however is concerned with the main divisions, and these can be located at the end of the second year (end of the initial spurt of muscular growth), at six years (marked slowing-down of growth, which will now retain the same characteristics until maturity), and at ten to twelve years (beginning of sexual maturation, involving a spurt of general body growth). These divisions have no clear significance for behaviour, but they are so apparent and cause so much physiological change that they cannot be passed over. They will provide the first landmarks in this survey.

Stages in the development of intellect and drives

The principal stages in intellectual development and the evolution of drives have already been discussed. According to Piaget, the end of the second year marks the end of the sensori-motor stage and the beginning of operational intelligence, which is first concrete and then formal. With few exceptions the earlier divisions appear again, but this time they are determined by an internal evolution which does not immediately seem to be related to bodily growth.

Similarly with the Freudian concepts, if they are retained as guide-lines. The period up to the end of the second year is taken up by the pre-genital stages which together constitute infantile sexuality. The period between three and six years is the genital stage, in which the conflict of the Oedipus complex is thought to develop. The next period, until ten or twelve years, is the latency period, which is followed by a rapid adaptation to adult drives centred on true genital activity. Thus the previous divisions emerge once again.

Changes in status

The stages distinguished above depend, in broad terms, upon maturation – directly somatic in the first case, intellectual or affective in the second. The environment appears to play a secondary role. It can of course restrict or hinder development, but it cannot actually accelerate it or create something out of nothing. Poor nourishment may undermine growth, and an adverse family environment may thwart intelligence or distort emotional development. But the best care in the world will not make a child tall when his height is limited by heredity, and Smedlund's experiments have shown that systematic training will not enable a child to grasp the principle of conservation earlier than the age at which it normally appears.

Nevertheless, many authors have proposed divisions founded not on internal growth but on the demands – particularly the social demands – of the environment. These authors observe that social status varies with age, and that it is change of status which is important rather than the physical changes which bring it about. The child who does not walk or talk occupies the status of the young baby in the series. This status involves a certain type of behaviour on the part of adults, particularly his parents. For instance it would be unthinkable in our society to strike a young baby, even if he were 'naughty'. These social standards, which are usually unstated but can be defined without much difficulty, distinguish this stage clearly from the next one. Between the ages of three and five or six the child's status is negatively determined by the fact that he does not yet go to a 'proper' school and therefore has the right to play all day long. He can move a little way outside the circle of his home, escaping briefly from parental protection, and mix with other groups of children in the neighbourhood, but he stays within a limited radius more or less within earshot. He then attains the status of a schoolboy, and shortly afterwards that of an adolescent. (From thirteen to nineteen, the teenager occupies a privileged position in our society, which involves a certain way of dressing and talking and particular rituals which the adult, inevitably, regards with suspicion.)

Seen in this perspective, the major divisions vary with different societies, but they are always dependent on social standards.

'Arbitrary' divisions

One can take one's choice among these different approaches. Each perspective is legitimate, and the phases of evolution are not clear-cut enough to suggest a natural framework. We are thus completely free to make our own choice, and to define a suitable terminology, without expecting it to be scrupulously observed by other authors. The Western mind has a certain weakness for threefold divisions, and, in deference to this tradition, I shall retain the three main periods of *infancy* (the first two years), *school age* (from three to eleven, through the whole period when children are not usually separated into specialised groups or 'streams') and *adolescence*.

Each of these main periods has its sub-divisions. In principle these are three: one representing a preparatory stage, the second maturity, and the third the stage where the functions become automatic and to some degree specialised. This threefold division was suggested by the German psychologist and teacher Kroh. For the sake of clarity I shall call these sub-divisions 'ages'. We then have the following stages:

1 Infancy   (a) the age of the newborn
                      (b) the age of the young baby
                      (c) the age of early language
2 School age (a) early childhood
                      (b) childhood realism
                      (c) the age of the first choices
3 Adolescence (a) puberty or the spurt of growth
                      (b) the age of enlightenment
                      (c) the age of vital choices

The idea of the developmental task

Although the divisions adopted are somewhat arbitrary, and the terminology more expedient than universal, nevertheless the content and presentation of the various stages is important. Most authors are content simply to describe 'what happens', in a certain order which focuses first on indications of physical growth or important bodily phenomena, and then on the development of intelligence and of the usual concepts, finishing with observations on very general concepts such as 'time' and 'God'. This is the plan followed by Gesell in his three books: *Infant and child in the culture of today* (1940), *The child from five to ten* (1946) and *Youth, the years from ten to sixteen* (1956) and more recently by one of the 'classics' of the discipline, the manual by Mussen, Conger and Kagan (second edition 1963). However, this presentation nullifies the development studied above, masks the decisive progress which characterises each phase, and finally robs childhood of its specific attribute – the fact that it is a progress towards a later state. A completely different approach will be adopted in this book.

In each phase we shall concentrate on the central *task* which the child must learn. Each phase will then appear as part of a whole, as a stage on a journey. To a certain extent, these tasks define the

evolution which leads to perfect maturity. Throughout childhood they mould the vital acquisitions which will make the child no longer a child and make him able to shoulder his responsibilities.

There is a further reason for adopting this idea (which is taken from Havighurst). It shows very clearly the dialogue between the growing child and his physical environment. As has been shown, maturation invests the child with increasing physical powers and broader intellectual capacities. But to each of these new powers society presents new demands, imposes conditions and obligations, and the child is faced with specific problems which he must resolve in order to proceed towards autonomy. At every turn society, the

43 The baby chimpanzee, although fed by 145
both mother surrogates, sought protection
only from the cloth 'mother' in Harlow's
illuminating experiments. Very early
conditioning dominates aspects of our
behaviour which would appear to be biological.

sphinx, waits to ask him for the password. She stops those who do
not give the right answer. She puts them in special institutions,
makes them stay down a year at school, limits their activities, or
sends them to the psychiatrist to be sorted out.

This approach has one other virtue. It implies that there is an
appropriate time for certain acquisitions. Earlier than this they are
too difficult to achieve, or they are not achieved permanently. Later
than this they are no longer possible. Organic development provides examples of this time-table which the organism must respect.
A specific moment is reserved for the construction of the eye. If for
some reason the eye does not form at this precise stage, there will
be no room for it later among the surrounding tissues, which will
have gone on growing without waiting for it. The same applies to
mental evolution. There is a time for everything: a time for crying
in the newborn, babbling in the young baby, having tantrums in the
child who is learning to talk, exploring the world in the five-year-
old, learning to read, write and do sums in the schoolchild, and
finding one's identity in the adolescent. If the task is not accomplished – that is to say, managed in a fairly satisfactory way – the
child will remain in some way incomplete, unexpressed, and
frustrated. The tasks which follow will be more difficult to master,
the final product less complete, and perfect maturity more difficult
to achieve, if not completely impossible.

This idea of the 'critical period' is receiving increasing attention
in the study of behaviour and of organic growth. It is known that
certain conditions must be present in combination at a certain
moment in the growth of a seed. If they occur earlier or later they
have no effect. The same time element seems to apply to certain
experiences. If the mother rat is prevented from licking the genital
organs of her young, they will not be successful procreants. There
are many examples of very early imprinting of certain signals, for
instance among animals of the same species, and these may even

include the signals which allow the smallest baby to recognise its mother. (Harlow carried out experiments on chimpanzees with two 'mother-figures', one made of cloth and the other of wire. Each had some attraction for the baby chimpanzee but there was a marked preference for the cloth 'mother', even though it never provided food; this reveals a primitive conditioning which has far-reaching effects.)

This, then, is an outline of the scheme and material of the following chapters, which will trace the journey of an imaginary infant from the cradle to maturity.

8 Infancy and its developmental tasks

Infancy can be tabulated as follows:

Age	Developmental tasks
Age of the newborn	Still entirely physiological
Age of the young baby	1 Coordination of eyes and movements, the first 'action' 2 Ingestion of solid food
Age of early language	1 Acquisition of language 2 Toilet training

Earliest (pre-natal) behaviour

Birth is such a clear dividing-line that the beginnings of psychological life are usually dated from it. But if behaviour alone and not internal conscious reflection is considered, it is quite possible to talk of 'behaviour' in a child not yet born, since he makes detectable movements and even *responses*.

This study must therefore start with conception. The Chinese reckon this in by adding a year to their age to represent their life before birth. This supplementary 'year' is divided into three phases: the period of *germination* (one to two weeks after fertilisation), the *embryonic* period (lasting until five or six weeks) and the *foetal* period (where growth is completed). Infants born before term are called premature. If they have not reached about 26 weeks of gestation they do not generally survive.

The first observable movement is the beating of the heart, a purely muscular phenomenon which is nonetheless impressive. Minkowski, to whom we owe a large number of observations on the reactions of the embryo and foetus, speaks of 'an extraordinary

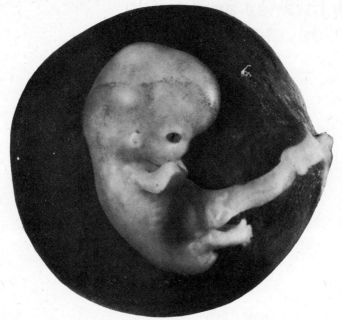

phenomenon: the poignant evidence of an autonomous life and pulsation inside an isolated and even fragmentary organism.' This has been observed from the third week. At about the same time spontaneous movements of isolated muscles are observed, preceding nervous control. All this is still only at the physiological level.

The mental 'ontogenetic zero' (Carmichael's phrase) must be placed at the moment when a stimulus acting upon a receptor releases a specific muscular reaction involving the activity of the central and peripheral nervous system. This can certainly be observed at seven and a half weeks, and perhaps at six. The number of zones from which one can obtain such responses increases rapidly.

The various systems of the organism are present and begin to function from the third month. The foetus, which until now has floated more or less passively in the amniotic fluid, begins to respond actively (we know this from clinical examination of foetuses spontaneously aborted at this stage) even in the artificial

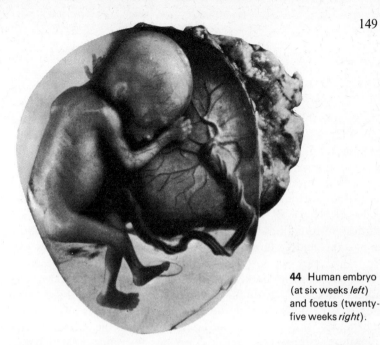

44 Human embryo (at six weeks *left*) and foetus (twenty-five weeks *right*).

conditions in which it is examined and cannot survive longer than a few seconds. At the end of the third month the foetus is recognisably human (see above). A network of nervous control is superimposed on the diffuse muscular activity, integrating it and making structured behaviour possible. Short reflexes, for instance the simple flexion of an extremity, and long reflexes, where the stimulation passes from the upper to the lower limbs, appear. The responses are rapidly differentiated. From the sixteenth week the mother feels the baby's movements. From then until the twentieth week the skin and the hair form, the mouth opens and shuts, the lips protrude and retract as in sucking – a rich repertoire of oral responses is prepared for the baby's use after birth.

Between the twenty-sixth and twenty-eighth weeks the baby passes the demarcation line separating survival from immediate death in the event of premature birth. We know the behaviour at this stage from surviving premature babies, who show how important the last weeks of gestation are for the maturation of behaviour.

From month to month the movements become stronger, the muscular tone increases, the observable responses become more precise, the respiratory rhythm becomes more regular, periods of activity alternate more clearly with periods of torpor, the hunger cry is better formed, and the sucking reflexes are consolidated.

The child who is born at term is therefore provided with a wide range of behaviour. This further underlines the importance of his earliest surroundings, the mother's womb. The mother's health is important, and certain illnesses which have no consequences for the adult may seriously affect the development of the foetus. However, it is the mother's emotional state which most strongly affects the early stages of life. The emotions have physical repercussions on the body through the emission of hormones or chemical substances which change the composition of the blood. These alterations apparently break through the functional barrier between the maternal organism and that of the foetus. It has been shown that strong emotion in the mother increases the activity of the foetus (movement is increased several times over), and that if the emotional state continues the level of activity remains high over a long period. Colic in newborn babies has sometimes been attributed to such causes. Finally, mothers who experience much tension during pregnancy often have a difficult labour.

The age of the newborn

The baby's education starts the moment he is born. It has been said that the whole of life must be coloured by this very first impression, and that there is a great gulf between the first impression of a baby born in a primitive society in a hut on an animal skin wet with dew and that of a baby born in an air-conditioned maternity home, where he is immediately taken by the expert gloved hands of a nurse and put into a warm bath. Certainly children who have a

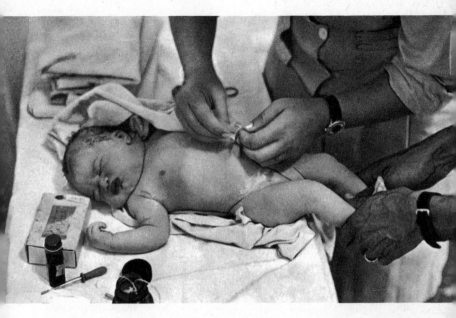

difficult birth, and sustain brain damage, sometimes suffer for a long time from the effects of these few minutes. Babies who cannot breathe straight away (and therefore experience a long moment of anoxia or oxygen deficiency) are less sensitive to pain in the first days of life, slower in the coordination of movements, and respond poorly to visual signals. At the age of three years they still have difficulty in conceptualising, and their IQ is several points below average.

Even babies who have an uncomplicated birth show marked individual differences. The boys move a little more vigorously than the girls. Among both sexes, some babies are more active than others. These differences may also evoke different attitudes from the parents, according to what they expect of the baby. An irritable mother will punish an active child more than a phlegmatic one. A father with sporting ambitions, on the other hand, will be disappointed if his child is too placid but delighted if he is excitable.

The same is true for the signals which release the baby's activity. Reactivity varies, in that some babies need stronger signals than others to make them respond. Some babies also vary their responses to a given signal more rapidly than others. In situations of tension, children react physiologically in different ways, some by a gastro-intestinal reaction, some by cutaneous phenomena, some through the respiratory system, some through the cardio-vascular system.

We do not know precisely which of these differences are 'directive' in having a determining effect on other traits in the personality, and which are secondary or transitory. However, from their combination an 'impression' of the baby is received. Notes on the personalities of thirty-one babies in the first months have been compared with notes made later between three and six years. The correspondence was much higher than one would have expected to find by chance. This confirms the very early impression many mothers have of the individual personality of their baby. Longitudinal studies such as that of Meili have examined these problems of personality difference very closely, and still have much to teach us.

Anyone who has ever watched a very small baby knows that he is hardly ever still, even when sleeping. He shows continuous unco-ordinated and pulsating (*athetotic*) movements which are usually 'segmentary' (they seem to involve one part of the organism independently of the rest), and of which the rhythm periodically intensifies to lead to a state of general agitation or to end in crying. From this background of diffuse motor activity certain clear kinetic patterns emerge – the reflex cycles, which usually concern one of the vital functions of feeding, evacuation or self-defence. As regards stimuli, we do not really know how much the baby sees.

It has been claimed that he only sees vague, general pictures, which will later crystallise into definite objects. Recent studies with specially-made apparatus (figure 46) have on the whole supported this idea, which is more theoretical (i.e. dictated by theoretical choices) than experimental. We know that the baby reacts to differences in the intensity of light (the pupillary reflex) and follows a coloured object after the first fifteen days, thus being able to distinguish colour, and that convergence of the eyes (involving fine coordination of six groups of muscles which regulate the movement of the eyeballs) is achieved on the first day of life, but that fixation of the eye is not fully achieved until the end of the first month. There seems to be a very early preference for *structured*, *complex* and *varied* stimuli (figure 47).

Opinion varies as to when this first phase of life is over. Some experts claim that it ends at ten days, others at a month. It would be useful to agree on a definite period, so that observations made in different countries and different societies could be compared. However, dates have very little meaning in development, even at the earliest stage. Birth only *appears* to be the same dividing-line for all babies: its distance from conception varies, and a few days in either direction are important because of the intensive growth, particularly in the myelination of the nerve fibres, in the foetal period and in the first days of life. It is better to abandon rigid chronological divisions and measure childhood by milestones which are significant in psychological terms. The milestone adopted here is the baby's first smile, bringing us to the next 'age'.

The age of the young baby

Developmental tasks
1 Coordination of eyes and movements, the first 'action'
2 Ingestion of solid food

46 The Fantz apparatus enables the reactions of the very young baby to different sensory stimulations to be studied and photographed. Here, the baby's eye movements in reaction to the three versions of figure 47 are being timed.

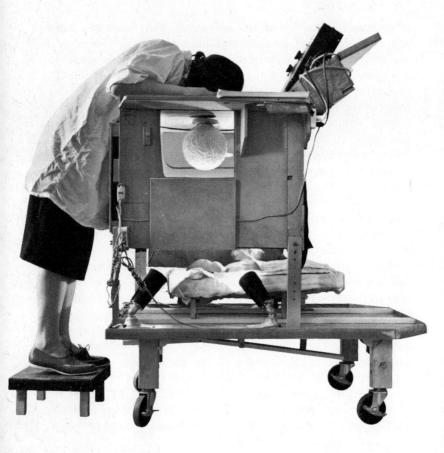

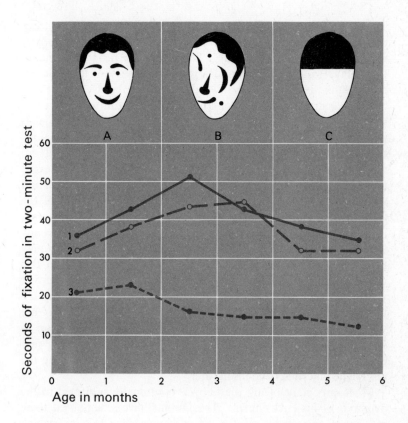

47 At a very early age the baby shows a preference for complex and structured stimuli ; the simplest image, C, is focused on for a much shorter time than A and B.

This age takes up the first year. Gesell has divided it into a series of maturational stages: 4 weeks, 16 weeks, 28 weeks, 40 weeks, and the first birthday. His admirable films show the progress achieved from stage to stage by juxtaposing in the same shot the different movements the child makes towards the same object – a cube or a bottle. The progress is systematic. There are fourteen stages in learning to walk, and ten in learning to grasp. Development takes place 'from head to tail', in what is called a cephalocaudal direction: the first actions to be perfected are the movement of the head and the fixation of the eyes; then eye-hand coordination is achieved; then the legs gain strength and allow the baby to stand upright and walk. In walking, coordination of the arms precedes that of the legs. Development also takes place in a 'proximodistal' direction, from the centre of the body towards the extremities: when the baby tries to reach an object, the shoulders and elbows come into play before the wrists and fingers. If two fairly distant stages in this development, for instance the first month and the end of the first year, are compared, the most striking progress is in the way the baby spends his time. At the beginning, four-fifths of the day are spent asleep; at the end more than half the time is taken up in activity. In the course of this year the child has had his first illnesses and has produced his own anti-bodies, after using up the reserve he inherited from his mother.

Most important of all, the baby is continually subjected to the demands of his environment. The Dubins have schematised these influences and suggested the chart shown in figure 48, which summarises in detail the findings of other research. In our society the baby is often breast-fed for a much shorter time than was usual in earlier societies. He is made to drink from a cup after the first six months, and is already subjected to some degree of toilet training. Social pressure is therefore already felt. While physiological growth (shown in a striking increase of height and weight) continues on its own level, the baby is already making progress on the social level. He develops in a climate of interaction with other people (at this stage mainly the mother, although the father figures more in European than in American studies), and this is the backcloth against which the child's activity stands out.

1 Coordination of eyes and movements, the first 'action' We shall begin by picking out from this incessant activity the structure of movement in terms of external signals – in other words the achievement of motor competence. Perceptual activity is a necessary basis for this, but this activity cannot really be separated from the movement provoked by the perception, and it is the whole cycle which the baby gradually constructs through his manipulation of objects during the first year.

Meili has analysed the evolution of the first perceptual processes into four phases:

1 In the first phase, as noted above, stimuli of a certain intensity provoke physiological changes (acceleration of breathing or pulse rate) apparently without any other modification of behaviour.
2 Fixation then develops, and the clearer the object stands out from its background the earlier this occurs (as in the experiments of Fantz). Fixation is made possible by the achievement of sensori-motor coordination, which allows the eye-muscles to be guided by the perceptual activity.
3 The third phase is marked by the general effect of fixation on all motor activity; in particular, the baby follows the stimulus with his eyes, head, sometimes even his entire body; all other muscle activity is momentarily blocked, and globally released a few seconds later.
4 In the fourth phase, fixation is followed by a movement of the arms, then of the whole body, towards the object which the child tries to grasp, often successfully. These movements quickly become more decisive and vigorous.

The third phase is crucial. Meili explains the blocking of the muscles by the fact that all nervous activity is drained towards the

48 American parental expectations from their children. The lower diagram summarises studies on the duration of breast-feeding (in Western society), the time of weaning, and toilet-training. (Each dot represents one study ; the table may therefore also be used as an indicator of how much research has been done on a particular aspect.) The upper diagram gives similar information about more complex behaviour.

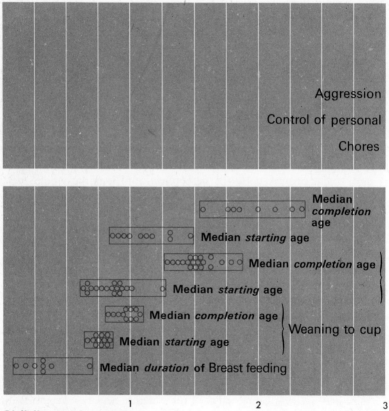

Aggression

Control of personal

Chores

Median *completion* age

Median *starting* age

Median *completion* age

Median *starting* age

Median *completion* age

Median *starting* age

Weaning to cup

Median *duration* of Breast feeding

1   2   3

Child's age in years

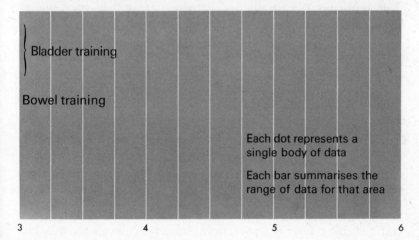

High obedience

Low dependency

control

behaviour

Bladder training

Bowel training

Each dot represents a
single body of data

Each bar summarises the
range of data for that area

3   4   5   6

perceptual sector, which is mobilised in order to reduce the stimulus and produce the first human 'work', a *percept*. At the end of this internal process activity is resumed. The films made by Meili and his collaborators allow us to follow this process closely.

The first effect of this perceptual process is that external stimuli are progressively neutralised. At first the baby reacts to every alteration in his surroundings, and when the signal reaches a certain – fairly high – threshold of intensity he reacts indistinctly by a physiological trembling of emotional origin. His reactions slowly become stabilised, and increasingly strong signals fail to elicit a response (they have been *extinguished*, in the language of habit-formation), while the signals which are still effective now elicit subtler, more adapted and more effective responses. As a second effect of this process, therefore, the baby's perceptual development constructs around him a world of objects which are located and crudely classified according to the action they allow him. From now on, as Claparède puts it, 'throwable things, suckable things, bangable things and takeable things' will increasingly make up his day-to-day world.

In this respect it is interesting to study the development of grasp (figure 49) and the postures and movement which lead to walking (figure 50).

This first developmental task seems to be dependent only on maturation. It represents the primary learning which Hebb placed at the very beginning of life. As such it constitutes the bed-rock of our later behaviour. However, from this stage onwards the baby's environment must be considered. On it depend the number of objects the baby can manipulate, the security with which he pursues this exploration of objects, the stimuli which surround him and the affection which is shown him for the smallest progress he makes. Maternal attitudes begin to diverge so quickly that differences can be distinguished as soon as the child is born, but in the first year parental practices are clearly seen to fall into opposing groups, first along the lines of permissiveness or restriction, then of warmth or rejection. This factor is important in the second directive area of the baby's development, his feeding.

2 Ingestion of solid food Biologically the child is dependent on his mother for his first food. The composition of the mother's milk is adapted to his alimentary needs. As in many other respects, however, what is biological in man is so hidden by cultural factors or so masked by individual variations that it is extremely difficult to tell what is 'natural', if indeed the question has any meaning.

Different societies between them solve the problem of the baby's first nourishment in more or less every possible way. Whiting and Child made a careful study of fifty-one societies. In the Marquesas Islands the mothers are afraid of having their breasts deformed and wean the baby as soon as they can without endangering its life. At the other extreme, a certain Indian tribe suckles its children until five or six years of age, and another tribe in the same region allows the youngest child to feed at the breast until puberty. The manner of weaning also varies considerably. In some societies the process is gradual and indulgent. In others, such as an African tribe studied by Geber, it is brutal; the time is decided not by the mother but by the grandmother, and the baby is weaned with an abruptness which causes him considerable distress.

The first systematic observations on industrial society, made just after the war, seemed to show clear differences between the practices in different social environments, the middle-classes being more severe and the working classes more permissive. Since then, however, these differences have not been found again, which seems to indicate that educational practices are slowly becoming more permissive.

However, if environmental differences may be disappearing,

162

49 (*below*) Grasping develops through well-defined stages, here illustrated following Gesell. The figures signify weeks after birth. After his first clumsy approach (at 16 and 20 weeks) the baby manages to grasp the cube, and future progress lies in making his hold more precise, until delicate manipulations are possible at the end of the first year (52 weeks).

50 (*right*) Walking, like grasping, moves through successive stages until the baby is able to walk without support. Numbers again are weeks.

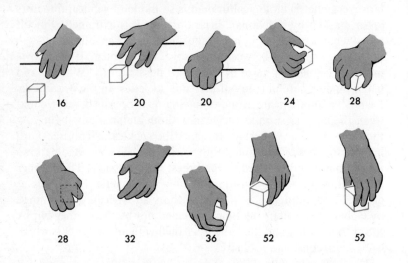

differences between individual mothers stand out even more clearly. The most precise studies on the subject are American, and the same proportions of accepting and rejecting mothers may not necessarily be found elsewhere. In one study ninety-one young mothers were questioned immediately after their delivery; three-quarters of those who had positive attitudes to breast-feeding their babies managed

4 (weeks) 8 12

Foetal posture Chin up Chest up Reach and miss

16 20 26 30

Sit with support Sit on lap, grasp object Sit on high chair, grasp dangling object. Sit alone

34 38 42 46

Stand with help Stand holding furniture Crawl Walk when led

52 56 61 78

Pull to stand by furniture Climb stair steps Stand alone Walk alone to do so effectively for at least five days (the criterion in the study), while the proportion was much smaller among those who had shown hesitant or negative attitudes. It also seems that women who are unsure of their sexual role tend to take the baby away from the breast, and do not let it suck strongly enough to ensure a constant supply of milk. They are eventually obliged to stop suckling the baby for fear of retarding his growth.

All mothers have to make a further decision as to whether they should feed the baby according to a set time-table or when he shows hunger. There are great cultural differences on this point too. In our society fashion has changed. At the beginning of this century, under the influence of reflexology and primitive behaviourism, mothers were advised to 'condition' their baby from the outset, and it was shown that such conditioning was possible and that the baby would soon grow accustomed to the imposed rhythm of feeding. The opposing school, of which Gesell was the main spokes-man, believed in feeding the baby only when he showed by his agitation and crying that he wanted to be fed. As the organism quickly regulates itself, the immediate results of the two methods were much the same. But the method chosen had a long-term effect: in the first case the child developed docile and conformist attitudes, in the second he developed a feeling of autonomy which prepared him to use his later freedom well.

The decisive factor is probably not the practice itself, but something in the general attitude of the mother, restrictive in one case, permissive in the other. Whatever the truth of the matter, the baby will be gradually weaned in the course of the first year. One reason for weaning is (as we have seen) that the maturation of the jaw-bones make the infant's sucking painful for the mother, who is sometimes sharply bitten by the baby's first teeth. This hardening of the teeth also allows the baby to eat more solid food.

The time taken by the transition from milk to varied baby-food varies, as does the abruptness of the transition and the degree of gentleness or harshness shown by the mother. The infant is sometimes confused and unhappy on reaching his first state of independence. The brief period when the two regimes overlap sometimes causes feeding difficulties, which are further aggravated by the mother's (or father's!) anxiety, so that mealtimes become a sort of tragi-comic battle in which the outcome is always uncertain. The way the conflict between mother and baby is resolved is important, because on it, to a large extent, depend the everyday atmosphere of the home, the degree of general tension, and even the relationship between the parents. However, it is particularly in terms of the future that this task demands a satisfactory solution. It brings the child to a preliminary stage of autonomy which will soon be strengthened by walking, it provides the basis for a balanced relationship with the adults in the family, and when accomplished without any lasting frustration it prepares him for the other tests he must face on the rough road from childhood to maturity.

The age of early language

Developmental tasks
1 Acquisition of language
2 Toilet training

The child enters his second year much more like the adult he will become than the newborn he has been. The rapid growth of the first twelve months has remedied the disproportions of his body; the arms and legs have grown more than the head, which has grown heavier and has reached three-quarters of its final size at the age of two years. This restless growth now calms down a little, and the changes take place in depth rather than in visible size. The cranial fontanelles close between 18 and 24 months, and dentition finishes

51 In his second year the child is already capable of many different types of behaviour. He resembles the adult he will eventually be more than the young baby he recently was.

and leaves the mouth with its first set of teeth. The baby is now walking more easily and will make enough progress to vary his walking activity – going up and down stairs, climbing, pushing and pulling (figure 51). It has been shown that these developments are not really 'learning', since the child cannot master them earlier if he is taught or systematically trained. Maturation – not only of the muscles but also of the nerves (myelination) – is the keynote here. The baby has now entered on a phase of active exploration, ferreting in corners whenever he is given the chance, touching everything, shaking everything, building an interesting and varied world around himself and already making his mark on it. However, his sensori-motor skill will not be perfected until he can to some extent break through to the only practical level from which human behaviour can be reached – language.

1 The acquisition of language   Boutan has shown that, until the development of language, the baby acts more or less like an animal; as soon as he begins to speak, he acts differently and solves problems which an animal would not be able to deal with, but he fails to solve those which could only be tackled through conditioned habit. The experiment is an old one, made at the beginning of this century, but it has not lost its demonstrative force and analogous findings have recently been made.

The child is now entering on a most important task which occupies a central position in his development. Degrees of mental deficiency were first classified according to the ability to use language (chapter 2). A person who cannot speak is not a complete person, which explains the strenuous efforts that are made to develop *some* kind of language in non-speaking children.

Through language the child will gain access to the higher levels of culture and communicate with other people. Language is the point of convergence of the two great human aspirations, the

Walks alone,
seldom falls

Seats self in
small chair

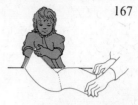

Turns pages two
or three at a time

Builds tower
of three

Fills cup with
cubes

Removes pellet
from bottle

Imitates stroke

Identifies one
picture

Hurls ball

On command
puts ball on chair

Kicks ball

Pulls toy

acquisition of knowledge and the creation of communal life, which form the substance of history.

The very importance of language, however, makes the study of it, especially of its origins, a difficult matter. It is not the business of any one specialist but of many. It concerns the psychologist, and also the sociologist, and, for the purpose of cultural comparisons, the anthropologist. It concerns the linguist, who himself may be a phonetician or a grammarian. It has become a special subject of research for cyberneticians, especially those who are attempting to make machines to translate or decode writing. To increase the difficulty, these different lines of research contrive to shed doubt on what was thought to be known about language, so that there is now no synthesis of knowledge to which all the 'experts' will agree. Since 1950 the structural analysis of language has revolutionised linguistics and completely changed ideas on the origins of language, and the progress of objective psychology has reached beyond the elementary mechanisms of habit-formation to the level of the most complex behaviour. In the following pages I shall be drawing freely from two chapters of Brown's recent book.

The principal stages in the acquisition of language may be defined on the basis of observations that have been made. Behaviour may be grouped into five stages:

pre-language communication (prelinguistic stage)
passive control
the first word
the first sentence
mastery of analysis of the sentence

The prelinguistic stage This category includes all sounds made by the baby which do not yet function as language. The first of these is clearly the *birth cry*. Poets have read much into this cry; to Lucretius (V, 222–7) it was a presentiment of the host of misfortunes which the new being would inevitably encounter in this life. The scientist is less imaginative, or less pessimistic: to him the cry is just a reflex, a sign that the respiratory mechanism is functioning in the air for the first time. The cry was prepared, however, several weeks previously, and the phonetic mechanism was present a long time before birth.

The newborn baby spends most of the time asleep, and when he cries this is still a reflex, a signal that the motor agitation resulting from his state of discomfort has reached a certain level and become generalised. The cry is not directed (direction will later be an important element in language), but it is effective since it usually causes the adults present to behave in a way that is gratifying to the baby. In this way it can soon take on an expressive value, but it should be remembered that animals are also capable of this behaviour, and that one important aspect of language, its *representative* side, is lacking in these first sounds.

From the moment of birth the baby is surrounded by a constant flow of language, which he himself stimulates in those around him. He is conscious of other people not simply as objects moving erratically around him, but also as sounds and vocal caresses. It is difficult to study the beginnings of language precisely because of the adults who devote their attention to the baby and constantly influence the situation. It would take great courage today to repeat the experiment of the Egyptian pharaoh described by Herodotus who had children brought up without anyone ever speaking to them. One can only guess at the exact circumstances of the first acts of phonation.

Every mother knows that the baby varies his cries. Psychologists have tried to make controlled studies on these cries, and Sherman's experiments are often quoted. Sherman isolated a number of infant cries and showed that the adults who cooperated in the experiment completely failed to interpret them unless they were given other clues. However, the experimental conditions themselves falsified the material. The cries had been reduced to the same duration, and duration is one of the clues which help the adult in his interpretation. The cry varies according to what provokes it. It rises gradually when the cause is gradual, like hunger, and bursts forth suddenly when the cause is sudden, like a loud noise nearby. Its rhythm varies with circumstances. In this way the adult quickly learns to interpret it. But although it is a means by which the baby can communicate with the adult it is not a real language, because it lacks intention.

Intention only appears gradually. At quite an early age the baby produces, as well as cries, spontaneous vocalisations which do not seem to be connected with any lack or need, but occur rather like the other uncoordinated movements of the newborn. These vocalisations are extremely rich in variety, and are certainly not restricted to the sounds used by the parents in speech ('phonemes' in linguistic terminology). An exhaustive study was carried out on American babies by Irwin and Chen. A sample of the sounds made by the infants in a given period was taken, the sounds identified were phonetically transcribed, and the frequency was studied. At the age of about eleven months the baby's repertoire is complete, containing all the sounds used by the adult as well as a large number which will disappear.

It is interesting to note that the profile of the infant's babbling with its corresponding frequencies is very different from the 'adult' profile (that of the infant's surroundings) at the beginning, and only slowly begins to resemble it. This does not mean that the conditions for intentional imitation have already been met. The explanation is probably that the sounds made by the parents augment the frequency of the sounds heard by the infant, who would not make much distinction between sounds made by himself and sounds coming from the environment, and that eventually these adult

52 The number of *different* vowels and consonants (i.e. the number of types) produced by 90 children was counted every two months from birth to two and a half years. (The fifteen such observation sessions are shown on the horizontal axis.) In the first year the number of different vowels was greater; after the sixth session, however, the consonants became more differentiated.

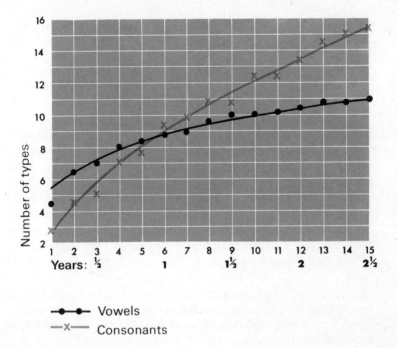

●—●— Vowels
—×— Consonants

sounds are strongly reinforced while the others are extinguished and forgotten. In this case the laws of habit-formation would not be called in question at this level.

Passive control The gradual approach of the baby's phonetic profile to that of the adult is hastened by an early coding process through which sounds take on meaning. At first the meaning is only felt passively; it is not yet spontaneously used by the child.

This progress is made in the same conditions as we have noted for perceptual activity. The baby now discriminates sounds, and understands several combinations of them. Ruke-Dravina, a Latvian linguistic psychologist, noticed that at six months of age his son looked at the push-chair at the words 'Iesim urru urru?' ('Shall we go for a spin?' i.e. out in the car). At eight months he burst into tears when his mother said 'Yai tu gribi nammu nammu?' ('Do you want a smack?') and clapped his hands in time to a rhyme

A critical attitude, however, is essential. In the early days of psychology Meumann asked his little boy 'Wo ist das Fenster?' ('Where is the window?') and saw him point to the window. When he repeated the question in French and then in English the child repeated the gesture. To make quite sure, Meumann asked 'Wo ist die Tür?' ('Where is the door?'), and again the child pointed to the window. It is clear that the child does not understand exactly what the adult has said. He reacts to the intonation of the words and to the situation, in terms of his past experience. The decisive step will be the first active coding.

The first word When the child attributes meaning to a sound he has reached the level of phonemes. He builds up his own repertoire of these, and it will gradually be increased. But we still know little about where this process starts and how the repertoire is augmented. Jakobson has suggested that the child starts with a marked contrast, for example a labial ('p') which involves the maximum closure of the acoustic tract, followed by a vowel ('a') which involves the maximum opening. This produces 'pa', the first meaningful sound. The child continues with successive contrasts, for example opposing 'p' to 'n' or 'm', or 'p' to 'b', in this way doubling his stock of consonants with each contrast. Studies encouraged by Jakobson's theory have shown that the vowel/consonant contrast is by far the earliest while the contrast of plosives and continuants (usually a nasal or spirant, 'm' or 'f') is also very early, that the contrast between various points of articulation precedes the

53 This figure shows how the different consonants the child produces vary according to where they are articulated. Ninety-five American children were observed every two months for fifteen sessions (horizontal axis). Note particularly the marked regression of glottal consonants, hardly used in English, and the appreciable increase in sounds appropriate to the spoken language of the environment.

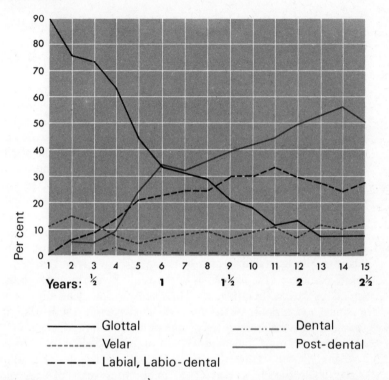

	Glottal			Dental
	Velar			Post-dental
	Labial, Labio-dental			

contrast of tone, that certain sounds, such as the palatal fricatives ('sh', 'j') and the lateral dental ('l') are late in coming, that in the vowels there is contrast between 'low' and 'high' ('a' and 'i') before contrast between anterior and posterior ('a' and 'u'); and finally that grouping of consonants is achieved after everything else (Ervin and Miller).

With this equipment the child encodes phonemes to form 'word-sentences', which then allow him to 'talk'. Children vary in the first 'word' they speak. (The term is misleading, because it suggests an analysis of functions which does not yet exist.) Leopold's daughter said 'piti' (pretty); others often say 'pa' (referring indiscriminately to any adult), or 'da' (which the English adult interprets as 'daddy', although it seems to have a more general meaning).

The first word is not isolated and in any case is difficult to recognise in the midst of the baby's exuberant babbling. The contrasts between phonemes give the infant scope to increase his stock. Velten has made a study of this, and states that at the age of one year ten months his daughter used eighty-six per cent of the words which were possible by her own method of word-making (consonant + vowel, consonant + vowel + consonant). Inevitably, certain words had more than one meaning. To avoid this, the little girl either doubled the words or made slightly different contrasts between the phonemes. The child is therefore obliged to elaborate his system of morphology because of the inconvenience of the homonyms. There is another factor which works in the same way. Before the infant can use all the phonemes of the adult, he substitutes another sound for the one the adult uses. These substitutions generally follow a sequence (Leopold), but as this early language is in a state of rapid development, different rules of substitution follow one another, co-exist for a time, and modify each other. The child often over-corrects himself. However, he eventually arrives at the adult system. His speech is 'correct' at about four years of age, and deviations (with respect to the environmental norm) which persist after this age should be corrected by the speech therapist.

There are many complex and conflicting theories with regard to the psychological mechanisms involved in the attainment of the first word and subsequently of vocabulary. Operant conditioning (Skinner) seems to be the main factor; to get something, or to provoke a desired reaction, the child learns to use an encoded sound as an instrument. However, this explanation is not entirely satisfactory, because we have not succeeded in getting animals to

54 The changing frequency of sounds made by the child according to his age, as observed from fifteen sessions.

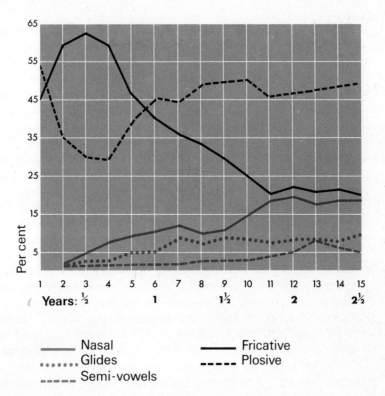

Nasal —— Fricative ——
Glides •••••• Plosive ----
Semi-vowels ----

do the same thing, although they are quite capable of operant conditioning. Vocabulary is built up against a background of actions which seem to be specifically human, and conditioning, by virtue of these actions, explains why languages vary so much with the environment. All the same, imitation is not the explanatory principle here. The child makes his own words, and only later does he imitate, by remodelling his spontaneous words on the ones suggested by the adult.

The first sentence It is difficult to make a clear distinction between the first word and the first sentence because they have the same function. Nevertheless one might say that the sentence exists as soon as one recognises *differences of function* in a series of words. Western languages have several ways of distinguishing the function of words; first the position of the word, then marks – phonemes which do not as a rule exist independently and which explain the function of the word they go with.

The first grammatical system used by the child has no marks, but there is already a certain word-order, so that the sentence appears as a telegraphic version of an adult sentence. 'That's the ball' becomes 'that ball' (Ervin and Miller). Braine has studied the first sentences spoken by three children. These children uttered their first sentence at 19, 19 and 20 months respectively. *It was not a copy of an adult sentence.* Braine made a list of the phrases used by one of the children, Gregory. Of the eighty-nine phrases he counted, two-thirds contained a group of phonemes which were fixed in the first position. These words acquired a function simply by their position, without any supplementary marking. Braine called them 'pivot words'. 'Bye-bye' thus appeared in 31 combinations ('bye-bye plane', 'bye-bye man', etc.) and 'see' in 15 combinations ('see boy', 'see sock'). These phrases can be formulated as type P (pivot) + X (a complementary class defined by the fact that its elements do not function as a pivot but usually follow a pivot, unless they are isolated). Among the phrases which do not follow this formula eleven are of the reverse type $-X^1 + P^1$, where P^1 is usually 'it'. The others do not follow any discernable formula, but they consist mainly of vocatives ('hi howareyou') or composite words ('mail-man').

These two structural formulae will develop rapidly and become more complex. The pivot words will soon become verbs, and the complementary class will become the class of substantives. However, this takes a long time during which experiments are made with the available formulae. According to Braine the child uses one pivot word exclusively for a certain period, but he uses it in combination with all the other words he is adding to his repertoire (after the second year this addition is very rapid).

How is this new stage to be explained? The usual mechanism of habit-formation can clearly only explain secondary structures; it cannot explain sentences which are constructed according to a formula. It would seem more helpful to think in terms of structured operations, following Piaget's ideas. However, the internal operation which is represented by the first sentence does not immediately relate to the child's sensori-motor activity. In this latter field, human behaviour is continuous with animal behaviour. The arrival at the 'grammatical stage' breaks the continuity, and any explanation which glosses over the resulting discrepancy is unacceptable. The 'neo-biological' concepts such as those of Portmann offer a more suitable basis for explanation, but they have yet to broaden out into theories more related to human behaviour.

The mastery of language The child's rapid progress in the mastery of language is marked not by the first word but the first sentence. Although we are beginning to know something about the beginnings of this development, we are still relatively ignorant about the period which follows.

Having arrived at the sentence in two steps, the child stays there for some time and tries out his new formula with all the words he has already learnt. New words are assimilated and integrated into this structure. Probably because of recurrent mistakes of expression, the child moves towards an inflected type of grammar, mastering the auxiliary phonemes which increase the expressive possibilities of the sentence. The first step on this road is doubling one of the elements of the structure: 'bird fly' becomes 'many bird

178

Sentence

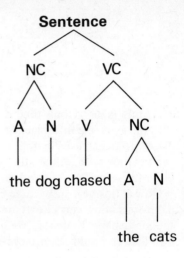

55 **55** When a clause is analysed, it is seen to be either a noun clause (NC) or a verbal clause (VC). Noun clauses may be analysed into articles (A), nouns (N), and adjuncts of the noun whose position varies in different languages. Verbal clauses may be analysed into : verb (V) and noun clause (NC), which last may be again analysed as above.

fly'. This quickly leads to the introduction of auxiliary words and marks, for instance the article ('the bird fly'), then the third person ('the bird flies') and the plural ('the birds fly'). These auxiliary words and marks denote function. Nouns are words that follow the article, verbs are words that come after 'can' or before '-ing'.

The child makes rapid progress here. Velten noticed that between 27 and 30 months his daughter made greater and greater progress in the use of prepositions, demonstratives, auxiliary articles, conjunctions, possessive and personal pronouns, and suffixes indicating the past tense, the plural, and the possessive.

The most detailed study (by Brown and his colleagues, Bellugi, Jean Berko-Gleason, etc.) is still in progress at the time of writing. The subjects are two children, a boy (Adam, 27 months) and a girl (Eve, 18 months). I shall cite only one example, which shows the mechanism of the child's progress.

Adam	*Mother*
see truck, mommy	
see truck	Did you see truck ?
No, I see truck	No, you didn't see it ?
	There goes one
There go one	Yes, there goes one

One sees from this how the child 'imitates' the adult, but *reduces* the correct sentence to his own formula. The word-order is there, as in a telegram, but he has omitted the auxiliary words. The child does not seem to be able to repeat more than three or four phonemes (his immediate memory is very short, as is shown by the Binet–Simon test). He must therefore ignore some elements of the adult's speech; he keeps the essential, but omits the separate class of auxiliaries.

However, the adult also imitates the child; this occurs in almost a third of the sentences used by the mothers of Adam and Eve. The adult keeps to the child's word-order but *completes* the sentence by auxiliary words, and returns it to the child as if asking for the message to be confirmed.

As the above example suggests, environmental influences become decisive at this stage. The child builds up his world of words through a continual exchange, and a profound difference will result from having an attentive adult available, or from only being able to communicate with other children who are as deprived as he is. All the comparative studies which have been made on children from different backgrounds, or whose parents give them varying degrees of attention, show that the children who have had most adult verbal stimulation are the most advanced. This accounts for the verbal superiority of only children, or children in the position of only children.

Of all the developmental tasks, this is the one which dictates later development and on which most light has been shed by recent research. It is not restricted to a well-defined period of time, because its various stages extend from the first sounds made by the child to the spontaneous mastery of grammar. It should therefore be placed at the end of the second year, which is the time when the turning-point of the first sentence is reached. The vocabulary, which at first is limited (an average of three words at one year),

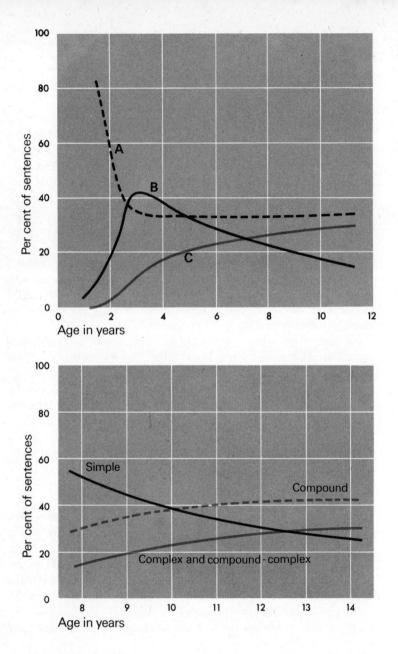

56 The relative frequencies of different types of sentences in children below twelve years. Curve A : functionally complete but grammatically incomplete sentences ; curve B : simple sentences ; curve C : more elaborate (complex or compound) sentences, i.e. with prepositional phrases.

57 The relative frequencies of different types of sentences in the written compositions of children between eight and fourteen years.

increases rapidly (272 words at two years, 1,540 at three years, 3,562 at six years). Language also becomes more complex, as is shown by Miller's two graphs (figures 56 and 57).

2 Toilet training This is a double task for the child. He has to substitute *voluntary* control for what was previously a reflex activity, and thus alter the level of the activity. He also has to submit a source of intimate satisfaction to *social* control.

Starting with the first point, the task may be considered as the insertion of new elements into a chain of signals and responses (Dollard and Miller). In the first months, the full bladder or intestine acted as signals for the relaxation of the viscera and the removal of the discomfort. This direct relationship has to be altered. Between the signal of heaviness or fullness and the evacuation of urine or faeces, the infant has to insert a supplementary form of behaviour, such as calling his mother or going to a certain place, undressing, and sitting on his pot, and he has to do all this without yielding to the impulse which had been so effective in the earlier period. He would only be spontaneously capable of this extremely complicated behaviour at the end of a long period of maturation. Social pressures hasten its acquisition.

This social pressure takes the form of a positive reinforcement of behaviour controlled at a high level, and a negative reinforcement of the original behaviour. This neutral scientific terminology represents the active role of the mother, rewarding or punishing the child. To the child, his mother is the incarnation of the social demands he must strive to satisfy.

Because of the tendency in modern society to accelerate toilet training, it is inevitable that the mother should punish the child frequently. A number of factors combine to reinforce this acceleration. One is the conditions in which we now live. City life tolerates dirt far less than country life – or to put it another way, the problem of excrement is different in urban society and in traditional society. Although it was certainly never a matter of complete indifference, the odour and sight of excrement and refuse was tolerated for many centuries in a way that contrasts strongly with the precautions we now take to avoid it.

This indicates that the essential factor in all industrial countries is the parental attitude, which is determined by bourgeois society. The care of the body becomes very important. Daily life is invaded by hygiene ('the religion of the irreligious'), and so, naturally, is the life of the infant. The mother is anxious that her child should be 'clean'. Very early, too early, she demands this of him, in such a way that relapses are inevitable. They are felt all the more keenly if the child had at first seemed to be controlling himself. The punishment is not always physical, of course; it often consists of appearing disgusted, speaking reprovingly to the child, or refusing to have anything to do with him for a time, which he is bound to feel as a withdrawal of affection. Praise, when deserved, is correspondingly excessive; the parents' joy over their offspring's 'work' shows the importance they attach to it. In these circumstances it is easy to see how, in psychoanalytical terms, excrement comes to symbolise something valuable like jewellery or a bank account.

The balance sheet of rewards and punishments is mainly on the debit side. The child finds himself faced with adult restrictions in quite a new way. The adult has already appeared as a source of privation at the weaning stage, but alimentary satisfaction can be obtained in other ways. In this latest struggle, however, the adult seems to demand unconditional surrender every time. He is a more powerful figure than he has been before.

This situation clarifies what the child has to do to master this task: he must be able to give the adult what he so insistently demands. In doing so he balances what he receives from the adult in other respects, and thus returns the affective exchange.

If this task is satisfactorily mastered, the child will approach the following tasks with a certain feeling of autonomy. He has conceded his first battle for equality, and arrived at the stage of giving instead of simply receiving. He now has a certain accompanying freedom of movement; he can join new circles of friends and playmates. He is ready to move on to the next stage.

9 The school child and his developmental tasks

This period can be tabulated as follows:

Age	Developmental tasks
Early childhood	1 The growth of self-awareness 2 The attainment of physiological stability 3 The formation of simple concepts related to physical and social reality 4 The formation of the concepts of good and evil, appearance of the conscience
Childhood realism	1 Learning social communication in the peer group 2 Learning the appropriate sexual role 3 Achieving a healthy attitude to his own development 4 Mastery of the physical skills necessary in games 5 Learning reading, writing, and arithmetic 6 Acquiring the concepts necessary in everyday life
The age of the first choices	The change of logic

When the previous period ends, the child possesses the essential abilities of man as a biological species. He walks upright, he uses his hand as an extremely flexible and adaptable grasping instrument, he has the rudiments of language, and he has a basic autonomy in feeding and bowel control. But heretofore, these achievements have been only a preliminary sketch of his later abilities: the next period will consolidate them and introduce new ones.

In this second major period of childhood height and weight increase steadily, the bones become stronger and all the systems of the body are perfected. The growth curves in chapter 7 show the progress the child will make in these areas.

It may be asked whether it is reasonable to place the child in a *school perspective* as early as three years of age. Many experts such as Mussen, Conger and Kagan, to whom frequent reference is made in this part of the book, call what is here referred to as early childhood the 'pre-school age'. Very few children in fact go to school before five or six; when they do they attend nursery schools in which the 'nursery' element is sometimes more in evidence than the schooling. We shall begin by justifying the classification of the ages tabulated above into one period under the heading of 'school'.

Since any division which cuts across the continuity of childhood is bound to be arbitrary, milestones which are psychological rather than biological or social have been chosen. A few pages earlier the age of the young baby was said to start with the first smile. The landmark chosen here is the child's arrival at a new level of behaviour at which he is *capable of being educated in a group of peers*. Each term in this phrase represents an aspect of the level of maturity the child has now attained.

He can now be part of a *group*. This means that his actions take account of other people, whether they are adults or children of his own age. This in turn means that he enters into a permanent exchange with other people, understanding the gestures and words they address to him and replying to them with more or less intelligible messages. In addition to reciprocal communication, group activity demands an early adjustment of behaviour from the child. He can only adapt to social intercourse if he has outgrown a certain childish clumsiness, the neurological basis of which has been described by Wallon.

This group is composed of the *child's peers*. As long as he was

only in contact with adults or older children, the child always had someone to protect him against external dangers and the consequences of his own clumsiness. It is a very different matter to be in contact with children at the same level of development, and in their company to discover behaviour which is unnecessary in the relationship between a small child and an adult – co-operation, disciplined contest, emulation, and aggression channelled into 'acceptable' forms.

Within this group of peers he is *capable of being educated*. This, as well as social communication, forces the child to restrain the 'intemperance of action' which was previously characteristic of him. The very small child is continually *distracted*, in rather the same way as children who have had encephalitis which has damaged

58 The three-year-old child is capable of being part of a group of children of the same age (his peers). Within this group he will begin his education under the care of a particular adult — usually a nursery school teacher, who will be a young woman.

the neurological integration of their behaviour. He is violently attracted by external impressions, spinning round in his environment like a speck of dust in a sunbeam. In the course of the third year his span of concentration, when he is absorbed in a specific task like drawing or making a sand-castle, becomes appreciably longer. This progress will enable him to start his schooling.

One more feature is important here: the appearance of an *educator*.

In the earlier developmental tasks the child knew an adult as someone who regulated his behaviour or suggested his games. The mother plays this role from the very beginning, and in Europe the father soon follows her. What is new at this stage is that an adult *specialises* in the role. Reference to past or more primitive societies shows that this role in its practical aspects is fairly recent, and is closely bound up with the circumstances of industrial society. Compulsory education is a modern phenomenon. The historian Aries was astonished at the number of forms taken by education after the end of the Middle Ages, before it crystallised into the structure we know today. One of these roles – that of the kinder-garten teacher – is still evolving, and is particularly relevant to this part of the book.

The child does not start his schooling at one go. At the age of three, as soon as he is psychologically prepared for it, he can go to a nursery school for several hours, perhaps not every day, and later he can go every morning. Gesell advises that schooling should begin very gradually, but he speaks for all psychologists when he says that it should begin early. In his peer group, the child will not be capable straight-away of learning anything other than the social behaviour which he will need later to develop the elementary automatisms of reading, writing and arithmetic. But this behaviour cannot appear unaided – it needs to be exercised, and it is better to adapt the child gradually to group activity, even if this only consists of organised games, than to plunge him into it abruptly at the age of six, when his behaviour has become settled and his relationships with other people fixed. Nursery school also gives the city child a variety of stimulation which his physical environment at home cannot usually supply. It creates for him a children's world, when his home is too small and too full of adult's furniture to allow him to spread himself freely. The materials it offers are chosen to help him to become more familiar with objects, to learn to distinguish more colours, to recognise more shapes, and all this sensory education will help him later when he starts learning to read.

The period from three to ten or eleven is therefore sufficiently homogeneous to be covered in the same chapter, although naturally the clear sub-divisions of age have to be respected. The three ages of early childhood, childhood realism and the age of the first choices follow more of an organic sequence than the previous period. The first inaugurates types of behaviour which are carried to maturity by the second and rendered automatic by the third, which varies and integrates them. The developmental tasks of these ages will be described with this organic image in mind.

Early childhood

Developmental tasks
1 The growth of self-awareness.
2 The attainment of physiological stability.
3 The formation of simple concepts related to physical and social reality.
4 The formation of the concepts of good and evil, appearance of the conscience.

Between the ages of two and five the child grows steadily in the cephalocaudal direction. His head grows less than his trunk, and his trunk less than his limbs, so that by his sixth birthday he is an adult in miniature. In boys the muscles grow stronger, in girls a little more fat appears in the tissues. Skeletal growth continues steadily and the first teeth are now present. The functioning of the organism is gradually perfected. The child's behaviour is already very varied. His coordination of sense and movement is now quite skilful, and his table manners are fairly adult, even if he pushes his plate around and has occasional whims which provide material for the minor skirmishes of family life. He talks in longer and better-constructed sentences, often without stopping. He is clean by day and night, barring accidents or times when the daily routine is disturbed, or when the family leaves home. He can apply himself whole-heartedly to the tasks appropriate to his maturational stage.

1 The growth of self-awareness Psychologists disagree over this task. They are disturbed by any question which relates to personality, because there is still no unanimous opinion among the 'experts' as to how personality functions. Clearly, however, from the moment the child says 'I' he has entered on a new mode of existence, and plainly knows that he is the *subject* of his behaviour, capable of opposing whatever is not himself, and in any case always different from it.

Allport divides the construction of personal identity into seven stages, five of which correspond to this particular period.

a The beginning of personality is the exploratory behaviour of the young baby. The baby's fluctuating interest in his environment has already been described. He does not seem to know the difference between external objects and parts of his own body. Until he is about eight months old, he treats his fingers and toes as if they were not part of him. At eight months he recognises his parents in the mirror but apparently fails to recognise himself. (Gesell has made some remarkable films on this subject.) At ten months he tries to play with his reflection as if it were another baby. We conclude from this that the baby has not yet unified his visual

59 The father plays
a central part in the
child's development

191

image of himself (his limbs and his reflection) with the physical sensations which he obviously feels, because he cries when he hurts himself and laughs with pleasure when he is tickled. At eighteen months the child is still centred on himself, and his relationship to surrounding objects is poorly defined.

b The self develops from two factors. On the one hand the child discovers himself through his parents' actions towards him, when they address him by name and show love for him. On the other hand he begins to resist. He may do this at the toilet-training stage mentioned above, which is the earliest focus of independent and voluntary activity. His *name* seems to be the first identity the child possesses, in that it allows him to place himself in relation to other people and gives him a certain continuity which is not yet apparent in his behaviour. In fact at this stage he is constantly being 'de-centred' by his games. He is a rabbit. He is a horse. He is a doll. He says so vehemently. He insists, in face of the adult who does not seem to understand these metamorphoses. English quotes the example of a little boy who, as he sits down at table, announces that he is an Easter rabbit, and Easter rabbits do not wear bibs. 'What a shame', says his mother, 'because Easter rabbits don't eat custard either, and I've just made such a nice one . . .' At which the little boy quickly reverts to being a little boy.

The child's resistance at this stage has the same positive role and is fairly systematic. In girls it begins slightly earlier and lasts longer; in boys it is very strong between eighteen months and four years. The important thing is that the child does things by himself. 'Go away', said Scupin's little boy, dragging along a chair much too heavy for him and defending it against the adult who wanted to help him put it in the right place. Buhler explains this negativism by the child's discovery of his own will, and advises parents to suggest to the child what they want him to do in such a way that it seems to be his own idea.

c A repetition of the same process produces the next stage, which Allport calls the stage of self-estimation. At this point Ames adds an element which has been briefly mentioned here and is of crucial importance. Until the age of about eighteen months the infant reacted almost solely to older children and adults. Now he forms relationships with other children of the same age. He does this at first through objects – toys or possessions which the children quarrel over. By two and a half years he has progressed far enough in his relationship with his peers to be able to place himself in respect to them, and from then on his relations with them will quickly become more varied and more numerous. He will become a protagonist in the children's comedy. In this way he will also assume a certain role, the consistency of which will help him to acquire self-awareness.

d In the next stage, self-estimation overflows the narrow limits of the early self and encompasses, not only the child's name, habits and indisputable possessions, but his parents and his home. The problem of identification, which has been described in its complexity in the first part of this book, reappears. The child seems to be gradually filling up his surroundings, like a distending balloon. At first he installs himself in one single part of his body; he 'is' his right jaw, or two inches behind the middle of his eyebrows, or his trunk. By now he occupies all the internal space. The five-year-old worries about being mutilated when his tonsils are taken out, because even the smallest bit of tonsil is an integral part of him.

e Allport's fifth stage will not be described here, because it overlaps with the appearance of the conscience.

The growth of self-awareness involves a number of delicate maturations, and corresponds to a critical period of growth. Gesell remarks that the period up to the fifth year, which coincides with this dawning of awareness, is strained and difficult. The child's parents are extremely important in this phase: he begins by becoming aware of himself as the object of their attention, he derives his first awareness of his own identity from their behaviour towards him, and, seeing himself through their eyes (he often starts by referring to himself in the third person by the name they call him) he struggles towards the establishing of his identity.

The damage which could result from failure in this task need not be elaborated. A child who becomes stuck in the negativistic attitude will be fractious and 'difficult' for years. A child who misses the turning which leads to personality will be deprived of the moral backbone which would help him to walk upright through life. This decisive progress is sometimes hampered by the child's difficulties in establishing physiological stability.

2 The attainment of physiological stability Success in the preceding task depends to some degree on success in this one. At the age of four or five the internal regulation of the child's body is strengthened, so that he is protected against violent changes in temperature and against the physiological effects of *emotion*. Emotion is known to cause physical effects which persist long after the original cause. In the adult, this internal turmoil is controlled by regulating devices which are more or less automatic, or can easily be set in motion by the will. The very small child is at the mercy of his emotions and they shake him to his foundations. The mechanisms which will enable them to be controlled to some degree appear at about five. This is the most purely biological of the tasks to be considered. It is included, following Havighurst, to emphasise the global nature of growth throughout these early years.

3 The formation of simple concepts related to physical and social reality This third task is parallel to the task in the preceding age which ended with the child's first attempts at language. The

60 Our civilisation appears to hasten mental development. The average number of words in a sentence spoken by children of all ages in the earliest studies (McCarthy 1930, Davis 1937) were fewer than the number found in 1957 (Templin). Children now possess a richer fund of thought, which is expressed in more complex sentences.

essentials of this task have been outlined in the brief study of Piaget's theories in the first part of the book. This is the point where representative thought begins, and is rapidly enriched with symbols which, with the use of language, soon play a dominant role. The child's sentences, as has been shown, become longer and more complex. His vocabulary increases rapidly and allows him to possess, if not to dominate, the objects near him. In this respect our civilisation hastens the child's development. A study made in 1926 indicated that a two-year-old child knew 272 words, and a five-year-old child well over two thousand (the child was judged to 'know' a word if he could name an object when he was shown a picture of it). In 1957 Templin found a more extensive vocabulary and more structured sentences at all the ages studied. It has been suggested that this undeniable progress is due to the impact of radio and television on children from a very early age, to the growth of nursery schools, which take children whose family environment might be less stimulating, to the increased leisure of the parents, and to the general rise in standards of living which means that people are surrounded by more possessions. Fridan, a critic of American life, would doubtless add that the American mother has thrown herself into her maternal role to conceal her existential dissatisfaction . . . . All these associated reasons quite clearly affect the conditions in which the child reaches his intellectual milestones, and the symbols and concepts he will need to guide him in everyday life. These developments are paralleled by the attainment of the first moral concepts.

4 The formation of the concepts of good and evil, appearance of the conscience For the child, this task entails submitting his behaviour (and his gratification) to a norm, doing what obeys this norm and renouncing what contravenes it. The task has several aspects. First there is visible conformity, which can be established in overt

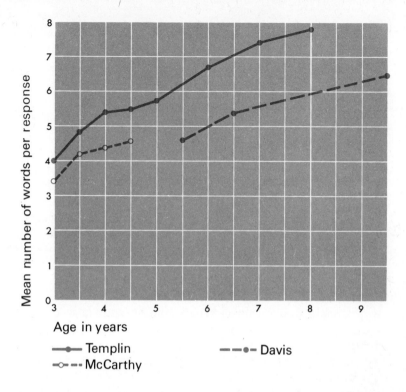

Mean number of words per response (y-axis, 0 to 8)
Age in years (x-axis, 3 to 9)

—•— Templin   ---•--- Davis
—○--- McCarthy

behaviour. Then there are guilt feelings, perhaps at first only after doing wrong, but soon ready to anticipate wrong-doing and prevent it. Finally there is the interpretation of these rules and guilt-feelings into moral judgments. This third aspect is usually considered to be the latest, the first two coming together.

Everyone who has studied the emergence of conscience believes that it is acquired, and is not the manifestation of something innate. However, there are different views on how it is to be explained. In the section on identification it was noted that Freud believed conscience (which he called the *super-ego*) to be an adoption by the child of the rules he was made to obey by his father, and thus of the moral code of his society. The theories of habit-formation, which are mostly American, have not generally followed this inverted mechanism of Freud's; they held at first that conscience was more a phenomenon of situations than a general entity, and later that it needed no further explanation than operant conditioning. On the first point, a famous study was carried out twenty years ago on the temptation to cheat in children; almost all the children cheated in one situation or another, but it was impossible to pick out children who persistently cheated and children who were persistently honest. Conformity to a moral code therefore depended on the situation, and not on an internal pressure automatically exerting a guiding influence. On the second point, it has frequently been shown that an animal which receives some kind of shock in a given situation will tend to avoid the situation (for instance leaping out of a cage in which the floor is connected to an electric charge). In the same way the child would learn to expect punishment, and would not break the rules for fear of exposing himself to it. The whole problem was revived by a fairly old study of Piaget's, showing that the child progresses from an early morality which is authoritarian and objective (in the sense that he is aware only of the fault itself, not the intention) to a second, more flexible and subjective type.

Experimental studies on this subject have usually explained conscience in terms of the child's actual situation and the whole gamut of interactions between parents and child, considering the factors of sex, sibling rank of the child, and educational practices and their implications. On the whole these studies confirm Piaget's picture of the child's early moral code, oriented to obedience and punishment, according to which a fault is serious in proportion to the objective harm it causes, and in which the rules are rigid (although little respected), absolute, and arbitrary. This is the moral code which emerges at this particular age, and will later become more flexible and subtle. If this early pattern does not take shape, there is a risk that in his later development the individual will find himself in increasingly serious conflict with his immediate circle or with society itself, until he is eventually trapped in some form of delinquency.

Childhood realism

Developmental tasks
1 Learning social communication in the peer group.
2 Learning the appropriate sexual role.
3 Achieving a healthy attitude to his own development.
4 Mastery of the physical skills necessary in games.
5 Learning reading, writing and arithmetic.
6 Acquiring the concepts necessary in everyday life.

Although the preceding age was classified under the heading of 'school', few children, and rarely the majority of the 'cohort' (the demographic term for those born in the same year), are yet attending nursery schools or kindergarten at this age. The obligatory age for starting school is five or six years in most countries. From then on, school becomes a universal situation and presents the child with specific developmental tasks. These tasks have been prepared for by the earlier ones, and will continue throughout the four or five years when the child is a 'school child' in the fullest sense of the word, defined by his school more than by his family.

Growth continues regularly, but its rhythm slows down a little before the spurt of growth at puberty. The child's body becomes more robust; at eleven he is twice as strong as he was at six, has lost his childish clumsiness, has his second teeth, and has greater physical resistance to illness and strenuous effort.

This age, according to Freud, as we have seen, is the *latency period*, when the affection the child formerly felt for the people near him is directed towards objects. There has been much discussion on this point. It seems clear that there is a strong cultural or familial

factor in some children's apparent lack of interest in sexual matters. In other societies there is scarcely any break in the child's sexual activity. Heterosexual play is a favourite occupation of children of this age, where it is tolerated by the adults. In our society certain families tolerate the child's questions and reflections on sexual matters more than others, even if they do not tolerate his overt sexual activity, and Kinsey, who questioned his subjects on their childhood, found that much clandestine experiment and exploration about these mysterious matters goes on at this period. But there is some validity in the Freudian statement. The centre of the child's activity shifts from sexuality to the manipulation and knowledge of objects. The tremendous number of new adaptations the child must make in a relatively short time also consumes a large proportion of his energy.

These adaptations are mainly on the social level (that is, in his relations with other people), but within the specific environment of school they are also intellectual. It is normally only the latter which are noticed. To try and compensate for this bias, I shall deal with

61 At eight years the child is in a true sense a 'school child', absorbed in the multitude of adaptations he has to make in a relatively short time.

199

the four 'social' tasks for this age first, and then with the two intellectual tasks (this time following Havighurst fairly closely).

1 Learning social communication in the peer group The content of this task has already been discussed: it has to be mastered so that the child can be educated within the group. Psychologically, this means that he must renounce some of his earlier behaviour, such as whining when obstacles are put in his way, demanding attention, clinging to an adult, or trailing close behind him – in other words, the various forms of dependence (page 90). On the other hand he will have to learn new responses which will enable him to cooperate with his equals, or to obey the instructions of an adult who is not one of his parents.

Some studies have been made of co-operative behaviour. It was first thought to constitute a totality opposed to aggression, so that some children would be 'co-operative' and others 'aggressive'. Newcomb's careful observations of children at a holiday camp showed that this was not so, and that the children who showed the most aggressive behaviour were also the most co-operative. Aggression and co-operation are more modes of contact than well-defined alternatives. The boys, however, continued to prefer a kind of universal aggression until quite late, while the girls, even if they had the same global score, tended to limit their aggression to certain situations. They also chose subtler methods such as verbal or passive aggression (not doing what they were asked to do). This difference between the sexes emerges clearly when children are asked to tell stories about pictures of animals (Muller). The task considered here demands that the child, boy or girl, should discipline his aggression in such a way as to strengthen the positive social relations of co-operation and emulation.

Similar progress has to be made in the relationship with the teacher. In most countries, and certainly in most schools, the child

62 One of the most important tasks
in the early school period is learning
to control aggression and to form positive
social relationships, co-operating
and competing without hostility.

63 In most countries, the first professional teacher the child will meet in his academic career will be a woman. This mother-figure demands that the child should deserve her affection and share it with the other children without resentment.

201

finds himself in the presence of a woman who performs certain maternal roles towards him; she helps him take off his coat, she praises him when he is 'good' and reproaches him when he is 'naughty', in this way steering him towards desirable behaviour, and she is often of much the same age as his mother. There are, however, two important differences. First, this substitute mother does not belong solely to him; she has to divide herself between twenty or thirty other small children all needing affection and protection. Secondly she presents him with intellectual problems which are usually totally devoid of any affective content. The child therefore finds himself having to compete for affection, and having to deal with unknown or little-known tasks which demand abilities he is not sure he possesses.

Faced with his peers and with this new figure of authority, the child does not adapt at once. He adapts gradually in the course of the first few years of schooling, and has more or less mastered the task at the end of the period covered in this section. The child who fails to adapt may take up firmly anti-social attitudes, or become isolated and wrapped up in himself (a disquieting form of unsociability in the view of the psychologist, but not usually noticed by the teacher because the child causes no trouble in class). If this happens, the intellectual tasks may be seriously affected.

2 Learning the appropriate sexual role 'How can anyone be a boy?' wonders the little girl while still very young, and the little boy feels the same puzzled surprise. The anatomical difference is so obvious that for a long time people thought there was a masculine and a feminine 'nature' which was only waiting for the right moment to reveal itself. However, before the discoveries of cultural anthropology Freud had already applied himself to the question of sexual specialisation. He believed that the child started as a sort of hermaphrodite, in a state of undifferentiated sexuality from which he evolved through a series of identifications to acquire the characteristic behaviour and feelings of his sex. Conflict between behaviour and feelings on the one hand and biological sex on the other (homosexuality) was a result of failure in this development. However, sexual anthropology alerts us to the very strong *social* factor in behaviour connected with sex. In the first place, this behaviour largely overlaps genital sexuality. Schelsky, among others, believes that social distinctions based on sex are to be found everywhere, from the most intimate behaviour to professional roles. Society allots social roles first according to sex and then according to age and family background. The fact of being a man or a woman thus has consequences on every aspect of the individual's life. These consequences are first shown in different parental expectations, and in the attitudes of adults to the newborn and the young baby. In some countries boys and girls are put in different-coloured swaddling clothes. The two sexes are differently dressed while still very young. They are given different toys. Most imporant of all, the adult subtly directs the child's activity into the behaviour tacitly recognised to be appropriate for its sex – the little girl is directed towards maternal attitudes, the little boy towards the exploration of things and noisy activity. My mother would not allow my sister to whistle, but the three boys in the family were allowed to do so and made the most of it. Physical (but not verbal) aggression is forbidden to girls but encouraged in boys, as it forms part of the difficulties for which their sex is preparing them. Girls are usually praised and punished verbally, boys with presents or physical punishment.

All this is preparation for the present task. The child must recognise and assume the behaviour appropriate to his sex, where previously it has been suggested to him by his parents and by society. This adaptation is not without problems. The aggressive little girl struggles to control her bursts of temper. The boy is often reluctant to abandon peaceful occupations such as sewing, which a little while before had been tolerated with a smile, but which now become 'girlish'. He is pushed, sometimes against his will, into rough games or an interest in mechanical things.

Social differences between the sexes, however, are slowly disappearing. This has been noted in the United States, and there is the same tendency in other industrial countries. Men and women now enter the same professions, as never happened in earlier societies, and within the family husband and wife, father and mother now share their roles in a way the traditional family would not have permitted. The same is true in adolescence and infancy.

Boys and girls mix much more in all their activities than they have ever done before. Jones has found that, over a period of twenty years, the amount of time young people spend in meeting one another (at parties and dances), and also the time they spend on their appearance, has increased, but they are also more studious, more interested in contemporary affairs, and more informed about social problems than they were before the war. The girls are more interested in sport.

This task has been the subject of many recent studies, and it is directly affected by present-day material progress and communications (particularly television). Success in it gives the growing child a measure of security among his peers.

3 Achieving a healthy attitude to his own development Here again, family training provides the groundwork for this task. It accustoms the child to the elementary rules of hygiene, and to taking precautions against extremes of temperature. This becomes a routine business for him. Scrupulous observance of this ritual becomes a matter of conscience for the child, as has been shown by analysing stories told by eight-year-old children (Muller). But it is still essentially external, something the child is constantly reminded about by his parents, and has little respect for if they cease to worry about it. For this task the child has to internalise these elementary rules, and perform spontaneously what he was at first made to do.

However, the task somewhat overlaps this framework. At school the child for the first time learns things which give him a foundation for this daily behaviour. He knows why he must clean his teeth, not eat certain things, and wrap up against the cold. From now on he has an intellectual basis for these habits, which reinforces them.

He is also brought to accept the rhythm of his development. The young baby overestimates his powers and thinks he can do anything. In early childhood he gropes towards a better definition of his abilities. Now, though, he constantly compares himself with his peers, who have the same problems as himself, instead of with his parents or with older children who have advantages over him, and he accepts his place as a child, accepts the activities appropriate to him and the division of interests between the adult and himself. Success in this task forms part of the childhood 'realism' which is particularly characteristic of the tenth year.

4 Mastery of the physical skills necessary in games An important element in group life is a certain proficiency in the activities of the group. At the primary school level the field in which children excel is not usually intellectual. It is the field of games – games of skill for girls, games of skill and strength for boys. These games are systematic and governed by detailed but flexible rules. Various aspects of play at this age have been studied (notably by Chateau), and its formative role for both boys and girls is agreed on. 'Directive' play varies a little according to the society. American society seems to suggest predominantly violent games for boys, and games requiring adaptability for girls. The difference is less apparent in European countries. Nevertheless it is important for the child's later development that he holds his ground in these activities.

5 Learning reading, writing and arithmetic We now come to the intellectual tasks proper, which the child is made to master in the next years of schooling. Each of these three basic intellectual activities must be mastered before the child is ready for the world of today. In the past, even up to the nineteenth century in the West, this was not so. On the one hand there was already a natural unwritten culture, and the child automatically became part of it as he grew up in the countryside. On the other hand it was only a few specialists who needed the 'three R's' for limited purposes. The state school is a fairly recent creation.

64 Mastering the skills necessary in ordinary games is an important task at this age. Boys' games are usually rough, girls' more social, and these activities have an important formative role.

Reading ability is determined by many factors. Sensory capacity (sight, hearing, and, for writing, kinaesthesia) is obviously needed. These capacities must be sufficiently developed to permit relatively fine discriminations. The child must have grasped fundamental concepts. He also needs a certain level of intelligence, a suitable motivation (wanting to read), a certain tolerance to frustration (to go on trying in spite of failures and slow beginnings), social maturity (for the teacher's help to be of value – see above) and reasonable health.

Let us take the last point first. Starting school is so often accompanied by ailments, colds and stomach upsets that for a time this was thought to be a period of childhood 'crisis' (Dublineau). However, it seems that it is only a crisis of adaptation to the new school situation. All the same, it involves absence. An English study (Douglas and Ross) on 3,273 schoolchildren between six and twelve and a half years of age showed that nothing could be done about absence at the beginning of schooling if the child came from a social class (i.e. the working class) which could not compensate for his academic shortcomings, or if irrespective of class he went to a school where the standard of teaching was low.

The conditions required for reading are only fulfilled at a fairly advanced mental age (page 25). Opinions differ as to what level is necessary. Thomson sums up the studies made on the subject and decides on six and a half years. In a recent thesis, Thackeray gives five and a half years as the minimum. Special studies have been carried out to evaluate 'reading readiness', and one of them, made in 1935, has been shown to have predictive value (see table 4). One begins by evaluating the child's readiness, and giving children who are below a fixed norm exercises in the sensory and motor regions which are involved in reading. In this way one obtains three groups in the first class, assuming the children are of the same age: an advanced group, who practically know how to read before they

start school and are given fairly difficult reading exercises to begin with; an average group who are taught the rudiments of reading; and a group who are guided through tasks which do not yet involve deciphering words or letters. Learning to read in the true sense will comprise several distinct stages, and there has been some disagreement about the most suitable teaching methods. Traditionally, children were taught to read by starting with single letters, combining these into words as soon as they were learnt, and then going on to sentences. The psychologist objects that this method assumes that what is easy for the adult is easy for the child, who can proceed from analysis to synthesis. In fact the child naturally works the other way round, first recognising the whole, and only distinguishing particular aspects later. On the basis of this argument 'global' methods were introduced, but they created unexpected difficulties for a minority of children (about fifteen per cent) who in spite of a high intelligence level were backward in reading ('dyslexic') for the first few years of their schooling. Teachers have therefore chosen whichever method they prefer without, on the whole, making any controlled experiments to see if it is really the better one.

The same uncertainties surround learning to write. This task will not be considered in detail, mainly because the role of writing has changed since the introduction of typewriters (unfortunately not introduced widely enough into teaching, at least not in Europe), and because writing has been relegated from the status of a privileged instrument of communication to a type of stenography which is mostly only used for personal notes and only has to be read by the writer or by people who know him well.

Composition, or formulating an original message in writing, is a rather more delicate problem. Although most children can handle language orally, very few can express themselves easily in writing. The schools themselves seem to be at fault here. They do not foresee how different exercises will be necessary, and, above all, they do not

Table 4 Predictive value of a test of reading readiness

Percentage tested	Superior reading ability	Average reading ability	Poor reading ability
90	100	0	0
80	100	0	0
70	42	50	8
60	31	56	12
50	24	67	10
40	8	46	46
30	0	12	88
20	0	25	75
10	0	0	100
0	0	0	100

usually provide the positive reinforcement which is essential to the learning of a skill. The number of words the child uses every day by the end of early childhood has been calculated as between twelve and fourteen thousand (parents are sometimes amazed that their children use such vulgar expressions . . .); the number of words the child will write in the course of his schooling, even when, as in America, this continues to the age of eighteen, has been calculated as a few hundred thousand – 4 to 500,000 at the most. The difference in the amount of exercise given to each skill is striking. A further point is that the child is rarely praised for what he writes. Most of the time he is punished (psychologically speaking), particularly if he is not academically talented. Thus by a cumulative

65 Reading ability is made up of several aspects : the perceptual, the intellectual, the emotional. Reading-books for very young children take account of this complexity, and thus make the early steps in learning easier.

effect he is discouraged from showing talent. School for him is something he does better to turn his back on, rejecting a jurisdiction which grants him no reprieve. He thus repudiates everything to do with school, and this creates a problem which has been sadly under-estimated – the problem of numbers of under-educated people (people who have reached the end of compulsory schooling without passing through all its stages) who exist in the demanding world of today like people deaf and blind, relegated to simple manual tasks which are becoming fewer with automation. Industrial societies must make a considerable effort to change their educational system and their way of evaluating intellectual performance, in order to raise the average level of intellectual ability. Rousson has summarised work in this field which shows that this task is perfectly possible.

As regards arithmetic, the child has not been as well prepared by the preceding age for what he learns at school. He may be able to relate numbers to the counting of objects, but he does not know how to use these numerical symbols. Here again there is controversy over methods. The best methods are those which are based on the mental operations involved in calculation, rather than just on the memorising of rules. This leads us to the next task, which is more directly relevant to this point.

6 Acquiring the concepts necessary in everyday life This task continues from the fourth task of the preceding age, and is subject to Piaget's genetic psychology. The child has now reached the stage of *concrete operations* (page 60). He has mastered reversibility on a basic practical level (for instance, retracing his steps along the road), and he is beginning to grasp conservation (particularly of weight and of groups of things). At this stage he also learns two kinds of logical rules which are important to school achievement: inclusion of classes and serial ordination.

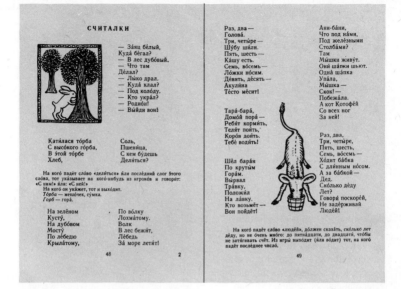

Inclusion of classes allows him to consider the parts of a whole and the whole itself independently. The classic example is the set of wooden beads, eight of which are brown and three yellow. The child is asked 'Which are there more of, the brown beads or the wooden beads?' The five-year-old unfailingly says 'the brown beads', because he cannot think about the material of all the beads and the colour of some of them at the same time. At the age of eight or nine he is surprised by the question, because he is easily capable of classifying an object according to two different aspects.

Serial ordination allows the child to arrange a series in ascending order (the second is 'bigger' than the first in whatever terms are chosen – length, weight, quantity, etc.). This ability is essential for the handling of numerical symbols in elementary arithmetic. The child learns by playing with teaching materials in which the numbers are represented by pieces of varying length, enabling him to measure the result of what he does.

The stage of concrete operations enables the child to manipulate the world of everyday things. He constructs and arranges objects, and often he collects things – sometimes only for a short time, but

66 With the 'change of logic' the child enters adolescence and thinks like an adult. He can now reason deductively, combine several principles to solve a problem, and work systematically according to a plan.

sometimes seriously (many stamp collections originate in this period). He enlarges his world, geographically and temporally. He begins to fill in the map of the world, and becomes interested in the past as such, although he cannot yet divide it into epochs. He makes plans for the future. He can save up to buy something he wants. In short, he is in harmony with the world, at close quarters and at a distance. Gesell refers to the tenth year as a *nodal* age, a kind of plateau of maturity in development.

The age of the first choices

Developmental task
The change of logic

Immediately after the tenth year the child enters on a period of transition. This is marked, on one hand, by the child's increasing mastery of the developmental tasks of the preceding age, and on the other by a subtle change of balance between the child and his world. Educators are very aware of the importance of this change. At the preceding stage the child, however boisterous, had been a model pupil. He wanted to learn, and he was ready to learn everything his teacher showed him. He is no longer so docile. He begins to pick and choose among what he receives. Some things bore him, other things interest him, and he neglects the former to devote himself passionately and exclusively to the latter. He also has a different attitude to adults – no longer the unconditional respect he showed earlier. He often defies authority. He 'answers back' (girls especially), he is disobedient, his thoughts fly off at a tangent. His personality defines itself.

This is not yet puberty. Physical growth has not started again; the child is still riding the crest of the preceding age, he has not reached the beginning of the next one. But in a way this 'pre-puberty' is already a step beyond childhood. The split will soon become apparent, but at the moment it is only a suggestion.

The change of logic At this intermediate age only one developmental task will be selected – the achievement of the formal logic of adolescence, which is a major turning-point in mental development.

This change has already been outlined. The child is now in possession of his thoughts, instead of experiencing them without understanding how they work. With this consciousness he can proceed to the plane of theoretical construction. He can reason deductively – that is to say, he can accept an event as being the effect of a law which he is able to formulate himself. He does not cling to concrete things as he did before. He can now solve problems which previously he would have refused to consider, like how many paws there are on three dogs with six paws each (when younger he would have said there was no such thing as a dog with six paws; now he accepts it as a hypothesis). He is able to use several rules in combination in order to solve a problem, and he looks for the solution methodically. He anticipates the result, compares it with the information he started from, and thus reverses his logical processes – and he does this without needing to use concrete operations. (From now on he only uses them as a secondary support, like an adult when asked a 'poser'.) He creates by himself the intellectual tool he will need to tackle the world of learning.

Success in this task depends to some extent on the child's intellectual level. Despite this, his school can help him to master it by its method of teaching. In America, science is taught by a new method in which the adolescent is left to discover scientific laws by himself. This method seems to produce 'transfer' (making other tasks easier to learn) in a way the earlier methods did not. This task, which begins at the age of ten or eleven, accompanies the growing child throughout his adolescence and is involved in all his later education.

10 Adolescence

This period can be tabulated as follows:

Age	Developmental tasks
Puberty	1 The recognition of limitations
	2 New human relationships
The age of enlightenment	3 Achievement of emotional independence
	4 The choice of the life-partner
The age of vital choices	5 The choice of career
	6 The formation of a personal philosophy

The three ages of adolescence

We are born twice over; the first time for existence, the second for life; once as human beings and later as men or as women. Up to puberty, children of the two sexes have nothing obvious to distinguish them. They are similar in features, in figure, in complexion, in voice. Girls are children, boys are children; the same name suffices for beings so much alike. But man is not meant to remain a child for ever. At the time prescribed by nature he passes out of his childhood, and this moment of crisis, brief though it is, has a prolonged influence.

For generations the picture of adolescence has been dominated by this famous passage of Rousseau: a moment of crisis, which separates the asexual child from the adult and has all the characteristics of a new birth, and, like our first birth, is primarily something which happens to the body.

For us today, hardly anything in this picture rings true. Adolescence is not 'a brief moment'. It is a long period which stretches over eight or nine years. It is not necessarily a crisis; there is certainly such a thing as adolescent melancholy, but there are also many happy adolescents – in our own society, not only in Samoa (cf. Margaret Mead). Finally, adolescence is not simply a matter of bodily changes, although these changes are the most apparent.

Maturation shows very different characteristics in different societies and different historical periods. There is of course a common biological theme, but the particular culture overlays it with such variations as to make it almost unrecognisable. Muchow has based an interesting method on this observation: he compared adolescence in successive generations or at given intervals of time. The universal factors were those related to the biological constant, but the historical factors were clearly dominant.

The most useful perspective here is therefore a psycho-social one. The progress from childhood to maturity is achieved by moving from role to role, by a series of turnings, most of which affect *human relationships*. It can be divided into three major tasks which are spread out over the whole of adolescence.

Adolescence is a time when the differences between people become apparent. Chronological landmarks mean nothing; each person embarks on adolescence in his own time, somewhere between ten and twenty years, and the later he starts the more quickly he emerges from it. Each individual progresses at his own rate. Some people move smoothly to maturity, others have to struggle towards it, some fight against this growing older, and others are in a hurry to get it over with and skip the transitional stages. Family conditions are different in every case, and school conditions in most cases, and the destination, the personality of the twenty-year-old, is always unique.

This means that it is less useful to divide the period into stages or age-groups than it has been elsewhere in this part of the book. Although this will be done for the sake of symmetry, it is possible to regroup the events globally into phases, beginning with the spurt

67 Sexual maturity brings promotion up the social scale. From his childish status, characterised by passiveness and obedience, the growing child moves to the status of a young adult.

217

of physical growth, then the period of expansion and stability, and finally the entering on adult life. The developmental tasks have deliberately not been subordinated to specific ages.

Puberty

Bodily growth at puberty is shown in the growth curves in chapter 7, and in figures 66–7. The child's growth seemed to have been exhausted, but it now starts again abruptly. For about two years it plays havoc with the stability established in the tenth year. Then this turbulent growth dies down in its turn, and the body settles into a cruising speed which takes it through the years of maturity.

In this flurry of bodily activity the masculine and feminine proportions are refashioned. The reproductory mechanism and, even more strikingly, the secondary sexual characteristics, mature in both sexes: in boys, the shoulders become broader, the voice breaks, strongly-pigmented hair appears; in girls, the hips become broader, the breasts develop, pigmented hair appears, the skin is slightly filled out by fatty tissues. At the culmination of this development the girl begins her menstrual cycle and the boy experiences his first seminal emission.

These two events are usually considered together, as if they had the same significance for both sexes. Admittedly they both establish physical membership of a sexual group. Also, in both cases, the growing child who is reconciled to his sexual roles and feels ready to assume adult sexuality will react quite differently to this tangible proof of his belonging than will the child who revolts against his own innate sexuality. Here, however, the analogy ends.

For the girl, menstruation is not accompanied by any pleasure – usually the reverse. The boy on the other hand enters maturity through the orgasm. The proportion of adolescent boys who have experienced sexual pleasure by the end of their fifteenth year is not equalled among women until the age of thirty-five. In adolescence, the biological pressure is at its highest at the beginning (between sixteen and seventeen), maintains this level until the age of thirty, and then gradually declines (Kinsey). The conditions of modern life, continually lengthening the period of schooling, block adolescent sexuality for almost ten years at the time when it is most insistent. This is further aggravated by the fact that puberty now starts earlier than it did at the beginning of this century. The difference on average amounts to between 18 and 24 months. Muchow has emphasised the psychological consequences of this acceleration. It separates and spreads out aspects of growth which in the past occurred at the same time. Physical maturity no longer coincides with the beginning of higher education (after fifteen or sixteen years in most European countries), with the assumption of adult responsibilities (symbolised by being allowed to see an adult film or to drive a car), or with the claiming of equality with the older generation (Debesse's *'crise d'originalité juvenile'*). All these things are dissociated. The body anticipates the other changes in social stature. This means that the problems of adolescent sexuality are posed in a completely different way. I shall return to this point later.

Puberty is a painful phase for all young people. It brings sudden feelings of sadness, of emptiness, of vague aspiration; it fatigues and enervates. The adolescent's attitude to his family is also very ambivalent; he isolates himself and stays away from home, but now, more than he did before and more than he will again, he needs affection which will reassure without hampering him.

The age of enlightenment

After this spurt of growth the adolescent blossoms into a young man or woman whose youthful grace effaces the earlier temporary awkwardness.

This is a privileged period for the teenager, a time of collective affirmation ('We're the young ones'). At puberty the child shuts himself away in isolation. As an adolescent he returns to the world – at first through other people, particularly other adolescents. He discovers different ways of living, he becomes open to experience, and he throws himself into explorations not confined to the imagination and the intellect. The term used here to describe this phase is the one applied to the eighteenth century in Europe – a crucial period of radical questions, of effusive sentimentality coupled with extreme licence, of passionate searching for the truth, of a taste for argument, of discovery and rediscovery. Debesse

68 The adolescent at last reaches physical maturity but maintains the exuberance of childhood.

suggested the phrase *branchement sur les valeurs* for this period. The whole world of culture is now open to the adolescent.

The age of vital choices

The foundations of personality have been laid in the effervescence of the preceding age. The adolescent is now eager to make a place for himself in society, to integrate himself usefully in the professional world, to take part in man's perpetual effort to dominate nature and build a civilisation. By a series of vital choices this integration concludes the period of development and inaugurates maturity, which is consolidated by external social signs – including in most countries, military service, the right to vote, the right to be elected, the right to adopt a child.

The developmental tasks are linked in a flexible chronology, more or less in the order followed here, but with occasional transpositions in individual cases. I shall not use the complete list suggested by Havighurst, but will reduce his nine adolescent tasks to the six which seem the most central and the most decisive.

The developmental tasks of adolescence

1 The recognition of limitations 'We do not know what we are going to be, but we know that we are not going to be insignificant.' This aphorism, often given as an essay subject to classes of adolescents, is more accurately applied to earlier ambitions. It is the child whose dreams are limitless. The adolescent confines himself to dreams he has some chance of realising.

As long as one is not in direct contact with reality, one does not know what one can do. *The level of aspiration* is unrealistic, and has little relation to the *level of possible performance*. The image which the growing child forms of himself depends on the adults around him, the idealised models he is presented with, vague impulses towards perfection, and, for the Freudian, on the paternal super-ego which he has internalised by a process of identification. This image now has to be put to the test. The debate occupies an important part of adolescence.

It begins by a dialogue between the adolescent and his body. This has been upset and refashioned in its proportions by the abrupt spurt of growth. But at the same time it takes a more definite form, which more or less matches the timid and always apprehensive expectations of the person concerned. Hardly anyone is satisfied straight away with the result of his development. Everyone hopes, however obscurely, to become 'the norm' – the boys to be tall and broad-shouldered, muscular, bearded and with a deep voice; the girls to have regular features, enough curves but not too many, a soft skin, fairly small feet, and medium height. When adolescents are questioned about this (almost two thousand were interviewed in one study), three-fifths of them say they would like to look differ-ent, and one in twenty makes really heartfelt complaints. Concern about one's body can be harrowing. It is the most frequently-mentioned problem when adolescents are asked to talk about what worries them. Skin troubles (particularly acne) can cause absolute despair.

These anxieties are secretly linked to the questions the young man and woman ask themselves about their capacity to attract the opposite sex and to be loved. Rightly or wrongly, they both tend to identify sex appeal with one or two specific attributes, and for a time they believe that their inferiority in these respects condemns them to loneliness. However, this search for a partner is not necessarily of central importance; it is one of the aspects of the continuous re-appraisal which accompanies the adolescent's assumption of new responsibilities.

The debate continues on the level of aptitude. Until he reaches

adolescence the child is working within an open academic structure. Although a large number of schoolchildren have to stay down a class in their early schooling, this does not have any adverse effects for their career until the age of eleven or twelve. After the age of streaming (eleven years in France and Switzerland, and the 11+ in England), failure becomes more serious. It implies a basis for selection. Further education is marked out by academic obstacles, competitions and examinations, which give the growing child ample opportunity to face external demands and get his bearings in relation to his former ambitions. The whole of adolescence is therefore dominated by a constant adjustment of aspirations following on actual performance. Children whose ambitions remain too high for their level of aptitude experience increasingly distressing failures. Those who aim low in the first place to avoid failure risk missing possibilities which would help form their character.

Lastly, the same dialogue between aspirations and practical possibilities is carried on in the field of talent. Many children will have started learning a musical instrument or dancing, or done well in competitive sports. The moment of truth arrives: is it worth concentrating on this talent? Will the child ever be good enough to justify practising every day, and perhaps making great sacrifices in leisure time and social life? Here again adolescence is a time of 'sorting out', in which renunciations are sometimes made which cause frustration for many years to come.

This task may be symbolised by the 'search for ego-identity' (Erikson). In this sense adolescence has been called 'the changing-room of the personality' (Debesse). The adult's eventual adaptation to his circumstances depends on a reasonable mastery in this respect. He will have struggled towards that *jouissance loyale de son être* which, as we have already mentioned, Montaigne saw as the supreme wisdom. The failures in this progress towards the self will weigh heavily against the adolescent's entry into adulthood, and perhaps make it impossible.

2 New human relationships A new attitude to oneself involves new relations with other people. The child stayed on the lower part of the ladder of authority or of Parson's quadrants (figure 36). His human relationships were both simpler and more superficial than the adult's. Adolescence makes the turning-point in these relationships, and this is without doubt its most difficult task.

As he ascends to a new social position, the adolescent has to reconstruct all his relationships in terms of his new-found sexuality. Other people fall into implicit divisions; those with whom physical intimacy would be possible, and those who are excluded from this, or are too old or too young. This categorisation crosses over the old scale of authority which divides people into superiors and subordinates. The social universe therefore becomes complex, and is further divided according to different situations – the family, the school, and between these the situations of organised or spontaneous leisure (such as the Scout group on one hand, the 'gang' from the same district or class on the other).

Each difference is translated into a specific kind of behaviour. The adolescent has to learn these minutely, like a new ritual, while making mistakes and slowly finding his way towards social ease. Runer has suggested a way of visualising this complex architecture of human relationships. Figure 70, for example, shows the social universe of Tess. The concentric zones separate the degree of social proximity and each corresponds to a fixed type of behaviour. In the centre are the *confidants*, those who are not separated by any social distance from the person concerned. They are the inseparable friends, to whom one tells everything, whom one refuses to judge in any circumstances, whom one supports in the face of everything and expects to do the same for oneself. A little further away are the *intimates*, friends or relations, rather more numerous and rather more casually befriended, to whom one would not dream of saying certain things. After these come the *companions* with whom one has no deep friendship; then the active collaborators (for instance people of the same religious denomination), the passive collaborators (people one meets in any collective activity), then the people one knows by name and perhaps by sight but has never spoken to. Along this scale occur the daily fluctuations of friendship and relationships. A face at college which one could scarcely put a name to suddenly becomes the object of love or hatred, a faithless confidant is rejected and drops down several zones, one adult gains the points another one loses. In Mary's universe, for instance, her father oscillates from zone 1 to zone 3 according to the incidents of family life.

These social structures are not innate. They differ with the society and the historical period. In our own society their role is magnified by the tendency of the adolescent group to unite against the adult group. It takes several years for the growing child to orientate

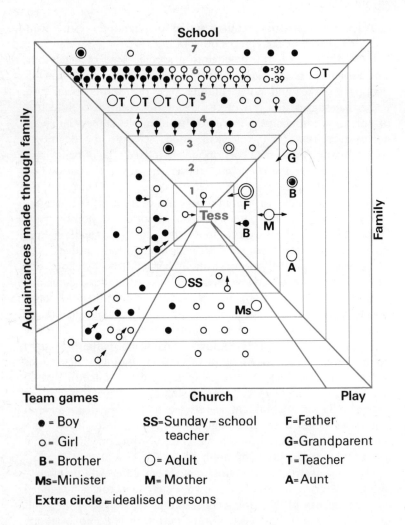

School

Aquaintances made through family

Family

● =39
○ =39

Team games   **Church**   **Play**

● = Boy   SS=Sunday–school teacher   F=Father
○ = Girl   ○ = Adult   G=Grandparent
B = Brother   ○ = Adult   T=Teacher
Ms=Minister   M= Mother   A=Aunt
Extra circle =idealised persons

70 The social universe of Tess, an adolescent. The plan is cut into by major segments, covering school, family, leisure groups, church and acquaintances. Every person in Tess's universe has a zoned place on the plan, at a variable distance from the zone of greatest intimacy (1). At present there are only two girls in this zone, one a friend at school, and the other a former 'acquaintance', now an intimate. However, Tess's brother (block circle, B, on the right) and her father (idealised) are approaching this zone, while the mother at present oscillates, further away, between the second and third zone. The arrows indicate whether the person is moving into a more intimate zone or moving away. This plan was drawn up on the basis of the information given in Tess's diary.

himself in this labyrinth, which no one explains to him and which he guesses about rather than understands.

Fortunately he is helped by groups which for a time offer him a certain security. From studies on this subject, of which Hollingshead's is particularly representative, it seems that the first group to form is the *clique*, a unisexual group of about five adolescents who are close friends, brought together by a common interest and a certain socio-economic equality. This is shortly followed, through the fusion of two cliques of different sex, by the adolescent *gang*. But here societies leave their own mark, and often the same psychological reality underlies less spontaneous groups, such as church youth clubs, Scouts, or charitable groups whose stated objective is a limited type of collaboration between adolescents of both sexes.

3 Achievement of emotional independence The child struggles towards independence from the moment of birth. He achieves it by completely remoulding his relations with his parents. This claim to independence has been depicted as a rebellion, a sometimes vehement negation of authority. The adolescent's emancipation can, however, be a gradual and peaceful process if he has grown up in a democratic family atmosphere and if his parents' attitude has been that of the educator and not the instructor. Studies have shown that strict discipline, involving corporal punishment, encourages children (by identification) to be aggressive and violent themselves, both towards their peers and towards the wielders of authority. The rebelliousness of children is therefore a function of the severity with which they have been treated.

This is a difficult time. The adolescent is 'betwixt and between'; he has outgrown his position as a child, and not yet attained his position as an adult. He belongs to two discordant systems of values. He therefore often presents the characteristics of the 'marginal' man – the *nouveau-riche*, the recent immigrant, everyone who is torn between two loyalties, like the foreman in industry. This gives rise to an irritability, a sort of anxious and exaggerated sensibility which makes the adolescent see all adult intervention as meddling and every suggestion as an attempt on his liberty.

Apart from this instability, the adolescent is in a state of total ambivalence. On the one hand he demands the privileges of the adult – a private life of which he will be the sole judge (which, he thinks, will give him sexual freedom), liberty to spend his money as he likes, the right for his voice to be heard in family affairs – but ultimately he wants to enjoy all this in a climate of irresponsibility. In the most important respect, economic dependence, he is still in the same position as before. Even if he renounces all checks on his expenditure, he can still rarely determine what he receives. For an increasing number of young people, education now prolongs their status as mere consumers beyond the age of twenty. On the other hand parents, sometimes openly, want to see their child making his own way economically, taking control of his own financial affairs, earning his living, and, in other respects, leading a quiet private life and conforming to the social conventions, which do not recognise the right to sexual relations outside marriage. At the very least they would like him to achieve equal independence in all fields, and not try to be adult in one respect when he cannot be adult in all the others.

These conflicting aims provoke personal conflict. The battle of the generations flares up out of small incidents of daily life, and the most violent arguments are often basically so trivial that a moment later no one can remember who started them.

Conflicts are not inevitable, however, and the new generation seems to be growing up in a less strained atmosphere than their elders did. Family attitudes are becoming more permissive, the accent is more on education in the liberal sense, and relations between parents and children are becoming more cordial, less tense, and also less competitive. The adolescent is therefore nearer to accomplishing the task of replacing his previous obedience with respectful friendship, and so of preparing himself to assume in his turn the responsibility of authority in a new family unit.

4 The choice of the life-partner Murray divides personality psychologists into those who only look at the surface and those who think it necessary to go beneath the skin of outward behaviour to the heart of the person. It is for the second type that this developmental task exists in quite this way. It cannot be reduced to a mechanical enumeration of behaviour which has to be learnt; it is more a matter of feelings, of something that goes on inside, and for this reason is difficult to observe from the outside and dangerous to discuss in objective terms.

A few pages earlier human relationships were expressed in spatial terms and placed in concentric circles. This spatial approach must be abandoned in order to understand the internal rhythm of discovery of the emotional world, to enter the area of intimacy where encounters are made which are decisive for the rest of one's life, or at least for a good part of it.

This deepening of the emotions can only come about through the

adolescent's new-found sexuality. But, as Chesterton says, 'Death and first love, though they happen to everybody, can stop one's heart with the very thought of them'.

In another way, this task is prepared for by childhood, by the sight of the parents' affection (or lack of affection) towards each other, and by a social and cultural conditioning which prescribes when emotional relationships shall be formed and how deep they will be.

Even so, it is a shattering discovery for everyone. Whether it happens in friendship or in first love, it tears down in a moment the whole network of habit and conformity and reveals new scales of values, and from that moment life is transformed, carried forward by a new impetus, taking its rhythm from the absence and presence of one person whom one is perpetually astonished to find so necessary. These secret places are often reached by way of friendship. Montaigne, whose life was changed by his friendship with Etienne de la Boétie, has expressed this admirably:

71 (*left*) Adolescent friendship often enriches the personality, and can be intense in a way that later friendships seldom are. **72** (*right*) Certainly there is sexuality in first love, but in Chesterton's words 'Death and first love, though they happen to everybody, can stop one's heart with the very thought of them'.

In the friendship of which I speak, [our souls] mingle and join together in a union so complete that they efface and lose for ever the seam that joined them. If I were asked to say why I loved him, I know I could only explain it by replying, because he was he, because I was I (*Essays*, I, 28).

This expresses perfectly the *personalising* role of friendship: it forces each person to complete the internal unification which began many years ago in early childhood; it makes the self, whose limitations have been proved in adolescence, a consistent entity; it validates the self by virtue of the love which the self now inspires. It has been said that the chosen friend usually lives in the same neighbourhood, has the same social circumstances and the same mental age. But all these factors will apply to many people and cannot explain why this friend in particular stands out among all the others. The friend is also a person, and not the representative of some category or other, and one suddenly becomes conscious of him as if he had been there all the time, only waiting to be discovered. Friendship is born of an incident, a chance encounter, a conversation which develops, a walk which begins like any other and suddenly alters one's life.

Adolescent friendship can take exalted forms. Often, however, it dissolves just as quickly, to give place to love.

Here again one could talk of 'heterosexual adjustment', and refer to studies which have been carried out on this delicate subject with adolescents who are skilled in concealing their private lives. Mussen, Conger and Kagan refer to a study (of 1952, but Kinsey has shown that customs change very slowly in this respect) where 582 college students between eighteen and twenty-one gave details about their love affairs. Among the men, four per cent avoided affairs altogether, four per cent avoided physical contact or only went as far as holding hands, twenty-three per cent went as far as kissing and superficial petting, thirty-two per cent went as far as 'deep' petting but no complete sexual relations, and thirty-seven per cent had full sexual relations. Among the women, one per cent avoided affairs, three per cent only went as far as holding hands, forty-six per cent allowed kissing and superficial sexual contact, forty per cent flirted more seriously, and ten per cent had complete sexual relations.

This is a superficial view. Love does not reside in statistics. Psychologists must respect this encounter in which a young man and woman commit themselves to each other as sign and sacrament of their maturity. Although this encounter has been prepared for by a long history of friendship, rough play, superficial quarrels and boisterous reconciliations, something else is suddenly involved. Those who do not know how things have a way of caving in beneath one's feet in the presence of the loved person, and of being drained of all meaning when that person is absent or far away, are the poorer for the lack of a formative human experience.

There is no doubt that first love is more decisive in our society than it has been before. It is becoming the principal basis for choosing a partner and marrying. Most societies have strict rules for selecting the people who will be permitted to marry. There is an Australian society whose rules would not by themselves authorise any marriages at all: young people who are attracted to each other go off into the bush, where they live outside the law for the space of a year. If they survive, their marriage has not displeased the gods. If they perish, they made the wrong choice. Perhaps this arrangement is one of those most similar to our own. Our young couples choose each other on the basis of mutual attraction. The high divorce rate shows that this is not an infallible criterion. But it should also be noted that in the course of this century marriages have been taking place more quickly, with people of more similar age, and are cemented more by companionship than by material possessions.

The American figures quoted underline the importance of the period before marriage. There is an ever-widening gap between the acquisition of sexual maturity and the time when society tolerates a full sexual life (in marriage). In the past maturity was acquired later (between fifteen and sixteen for most people, slightly earlier for the lucky ones), and the young adult married soon afterwards. There were fewer years of tension. As we have seen, sexual maturity now comes earlier. The moment of entry into active life is retarded by the lengthening of the period of training (academic or professional). The problem of adolescent sexuality thus becomes acute. At the same time, however, it is approached more openly. We no longer believe, for example, in the harmful effects of masturbation, which is being accepted as a normal stage (because of its frequency!) in sexuality, at least among men. But what are we to say about pre-marital sexual relations?

It is not easy for the psychologist to answer this question. He knows that the duration of a marriage is related to the length of the engagement, but unrelated to the presence or absence of pre-marital relations. That is to say, there are as many successful as

73 (*top*) Diagram showing the growth of world production from 1830 to 1960. The dotted line shows the exact figures, corrected to allow for depreciation in the value of money. The colour lines show the main trends : a rise from 1830 to 1870, a period of stagnation lasting one generation, a new upward surge from 1890 to 1930, and a second period of stagnation (the general slump) which lasted until the end of the Second World War. After this, production begins to rise again with new momentum. (The straight colour line is a generalisation.)

74 (*bottom*) Cake A represents the social structure in France in 1800 : most people earned their living by agriculture (1), there was a small industrial sector (2) and a service sector (3) about the same size. Cake B shows the structure of the United States in 1950, which is similar to that of most modern industrial countries today. Very few people now work in agriculture, the industrial sector is stagnant (in fact it is regressing because of automation), and the third sector is expanding rapidly. Our civilisation is one of services (the teacher, the film star) and large automated industrial complexes.

unsuccessful marriages among couples who put the pleasures of love before the wedding march. However, we should remember that a number of adolescent couples 'marry' before the socially-permitted age. In doing so they establish a new form of sexual relationship, which is not recognised socially in the law courts, but which public morality seems to respect.

In simple terms, married life goes in stages. It starts as a liaison, becomes official when economic circumstances allow, and children arrive shortly afterwards. In this respect boys and girls behave in more similar ways than in the past. The American figures show that the boys enjoy more freedom, but we are moving rapidly towards complete equality.

5 The choice of career The start of professional life is the crowning-point of adolescence, not only because it gives the new individual his last freedom – freedom of economic resources – but because it brings him into the largest human community, that of *work*.

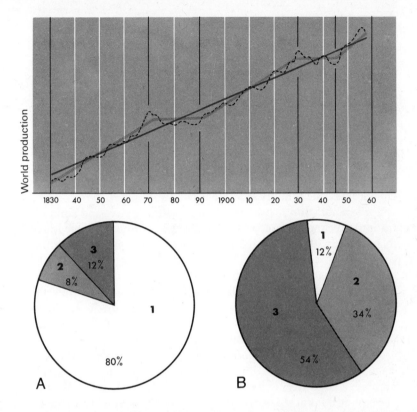

Work is an ambiguous idea. We must be careful neither to think of it as absolute (there are other human activities as well) nor to depreciate it, as Hannah Arendt invites us to. By work we mean 'an organised activity directed towards transforming the environment in such a way as to redress the lack of economic wealth we suffer, according to implicit or explicit social norms'. This formula brings out the *two aspects of work*.

First, it is an activity of transformation. Our distant ancestors who gave up trying to modify their environment are still swimming in the sea. Since the prehistoric emergence of man, the tool has been the sign that a new species had emerged among the anthropoids. Since the Renaissance human labour has become more productive, and its power is clearly manifested by the world we live in. In taking up a profession, the individual takes his place in the adventure of man.

Secondly, work refers to society and the social structure. The rise of the West (figure 73) was made possible by the social division of labour. Society seen from this angle may be divided into three principal sectors: the primary sector (agriculture, mining), the secondary sector (manufacture), and the tertiary sector (services and administration). Technical progress brings about a profound change in the relationships of these three sectors. The two figures (figure 74) compare two completely different structures. The first reflects the social composition of France in 1800; agriculture dominates overwhelmingly, there is a small artisan sector resulting from the beginning of industry, and a small service sector. The second illustrates the American structure in 1950: agriculture, although much more productive, is comparatively insignificant, the secondary sector, after a tremendous expansion in the last century, is stagnating (because of automation), and the tertiary sector occupies a large area.

These structural changes correspond to a considerable diversification of professions. There were less than two hundred professions in traditional society until the French Revolution. The first census of professions in England, in 1840, counted 440. In America in 1944 the number was estimated at 30,000.

The number of jobs itself complicates the business of going into the outside world. The adolescent is not well informed about the variety of careers available. He is only aware of those which are mentioned in everyday conversation and more or less represent the professions of traditional society. Everyone knows roughly what the baker, the woodcutter and the shoemaker do. But the professions of the last century are less clearly defined (many of them have vague names like 'workman' or 'engineer'), and those which have grown out of modern technology are often unknown (how many people know exactly what a statistician, a programmer or a meteorologist do ?).

Whenever some aspect of social life becomes too complex for most people to be able to deal with it easily, specialists appear. With the professions, in the last century it was the schoolmaster, more recently it has been the employment officer. He appeared a⁺ the turn of the century, and began functioning officially just before the First World War. In those days his job was to inform pare.... and children about the possibilities of professional training in the district. This is still the only task he is obliged to perform, but he often finds himself giving advice as well as information. His advice is based on certain tests which have been proved to be useful. In England it has been shown that adolescents who followed the advice that was given them after thorough testing stayed longer in their jobs than those who did not; that after four years most of the second group were in the job that was originally recommended; that those who had been seriously tested were getting more satisfaction out of their jobs than the control group; and that most employers were more satisfied with the work of the young people who had been tested.

The role of the employment officer is being changed by the fact that schooling on the whole is becoming longer. A growing proportion of young people stay on at school after the compulsory period. More of them take 'A' level or its equivalent. The work of the employment officer is therefore increasingly that of guidance, beginning very early in schooling and accompanying the child through all the stages of his maturation. The change of role affects the methods. Tests at a given time will probably be gradually replaced by regular non-directional interviews, which will give the child enough information for him to feel his own way to a choice of career.

The start of a career assures the adolescent of the identity he has already largely achieved in his relations with others and his first emotional experience. Modern society classes people more by what they do than what they are, and much more than by what they have.

The child's evolution seems to be complete, he now seems to be absolutely adult. However, something is still missing from the *exemplary* adult who was sketched in chapter 6. Evolution only culminates in a career for those people who put the collective interest first, without considering the individual's vocation for his personal destiny. For each person, this destiny is a question of the relationship he establishes with 'what transcends him'.

6 The formation of a personal philosophy Just as someone who has not experienced love or friendship deeply lacks something essential, so the man who has no personal philosophy remains this side of what he ought to be. 'Every soul which is well born desires to take part in the battle' said Rolland. Although only comparatively few people reach this level of human potential, this review of developmental tasks must culminate in the task which sums up and fulfils all the preceding ones.

Here the psychologist must give way to the sociologist or the philosopher. His science of behaviour describes man's actions, but is silent on the question of values. But childhood is a preparation for a life as a human being, a life which has whatever significance the individual gives it, and even the idea of normality has to be understood in terms of this significance.

The contemporary world presents the adolescent with such a maze of values, of contradictory philosophies and conflicting religious demands, that this last developmental task is more difficult as well as being more personal than any of the others.

There have been and still are certain societies which are firmly organised around a number of simple values. As the child grows up he enters a stable world and accepts the values which are shown him. If he does not he is remorselessly ostracised. This unanimity, at least in industrial society, has disintegrated. Our society is tolerant in that it permits the coexistence of different faiths in spite of the inherent contradictions of such coexistence (faith is a wager on the absolute, and there cannot be more than one absolute). There is no longer an 'official doctrine' of man's nature. On the contrary, as Scheler remarked in 1928, the only thing modern man is sure of is that he is no longer sure who he is. The growing child is thus confronted with the state of *anomia* (absence of any absolute law) which sociologists have recognised as the distinctive characteristic of our time. When he has to adopt a line of conduct and adhere to specific values he does so with fear and trembling, as a personal act involving him and is inevitably prejudiced.

There are six main streams of thought within our civilisation from which he can choose. (The 'messages' of cultures or societies with which we have no common tradition, but which have reached us as *possible* convictions, are not considered here.) There are three conceptions of man which are 'traditional' in the sense that they have a long history, are deeply rooted in the modern consciousness, and are still the inspiration of certain institutions in present society.

1 *The Judaeo-Christian conception of man, Imago Dei* The beginning of all things is God, who created man among other creatures, in his own image but fallible. Man broke away from his Creator through his own sin and can only be redeemed by complete submission to the divine will as revealed in the scriptures or by exclusive belief in God incarnate in the Saviour.

2 *The Hellenic conception of man as the reasonable animal* Here also man is singled out from the rest of nature, not because he is created in the image of God, but because he is part of the ordinating principle of the world, through his reason (*logos*) which is capable of understanding reality, whatever it is, and adapting to it through aspiring to wisdom.

Throughout the spiritual history of the West these two first conceptions have conflicted and been reconciled, but they are sufficiently close to one another and – more importantly – sufficiently hostile to the next one, to appear to constitute a single intellectual sensibility.

3 *The 'modern' conception of man as a tool-maker* Man is here considered as an animal among other animals, but possessing greater powers to fight his enemies and the menaces of the physical environment through his *technical* ability. In other respects he has the same vital impulses as the animal: he wants to survive, protect his young, and find sexual partners. This conception varies according to the vital impulse which is placed at the centre: there is the man of violence or of power (the *homo politicus* of Machiavelli and Lenin), materialistic man, racial man (various kinds of nationalism, Hitlerian racialism, black/white racialism), and sexual man (Freudian man, and man as depicted by certain important twentieth-century authors such as D. H. Lawrence). All these variations have one essential theme: the abolition of every radical difference between man and the animal, and the 'radical naturalisation' of man.

To these three traditional conceptions have been added more recent ideas which are less rooted in institutions but are formulated and vigorously discussed in modern literature, particularly the literature which is read by adolescents.

4 *Man as the dead-end of life* This conception is pessimistic in the extreme. It is derived from German romanticism, and has recently been fed by sombre forebodings about the impending doom of humanity, which will be wiped out together with all life on the earth by its own nuclear weapons. The proliferation of techniques, the increasing mechanisation of daily life, the insidious invasion of thought by publicity and propaganda, complacency in the face of contemporary problems, all inspire those who, like Klages or Lessing, see man as a fallen animal, 'sick in the mind', who tries to compensate for his fundamental lack of vital drive by intellectual effort. Fallen out of the tree of life, he is foolish enough to pride himself on his technical skill and his abilities, which in reality merely show his congenital incapacity to live properly. In this existential disaster man is recalled to his primitive vocation to live by the images of his dreams, by poetic creation, by the irrational joys of which sexual ecstasy is one form, and the effect of which is each time to plunge him back into a cosmic unity which he too often forgets.

5 *Man as responsible for the world* Some existentialists counter this fundamentally pessimistic conception with one which is fundamentally optimistic. In this view, man is responsible not only for himself, but for the state of the civilised world, and beyond that for the world in its entirety. Things admittedly exist, but they are opaque, massive, crude: a rock does not mean anything by itself, it is *de trop*, it only takes on a meaningful existence when I decide to climb it or when I shelter under it. The same applies to all things. All external significance is preceded by the effort man must make to dominate things and social conditions, and he must use these things as his raw material in freely making a human world.

6 *Man as a citizen* This conception is less extreme than the last two. It starts from man's animal inheritance, but does not reduce him to his biological impulses. It endows him with a certain responsibility, but not for the whole universe – simply and imperatively for the creation of an integrated society. It is through his effort to dominate his environment and establish mutual bonds of non-violence and reason between men that *man has a history*, that this history has a direction and a goal, and that the moral judgments that emerge from it are more than just a reflection of education or of the particular social culture.

There can be no obligatory choice among these six conceptions. Each person has to decide which one best expresses his aspirations and will organise his daily efforts. The educator can help the adolescent in his search by giving him food for thought and bringing him into contact with contemporary works which will force him to take up some position and understand himself better. On the success of this confrontation depends the ultimate fulfilment of the individual, which began with the first cellular divisions, declared itself with the first heartbeats, affirmed itself more strongly after birth, and has sought itself through all the developmental tasks of succeeding ages. From this moment another task begins, the task of every thinking man and woman since human life appeared on the earth: to live with open eyes, and to climb to the highest level of human ability.

1 Childhood's changing status

Baade, F. (1960) *Der Wettlauf zum Jahre 2,000*, Oldenburg: Stelling Verlag.

Bossard, J. H. S. (1954) *The Sociology of Child Development*, 2nd edn., New York: Harper.

Fourastie, J. (1960) 'Trois remarques sur le proche avenir de l'humanité, *Diogenes*, (**30**), pp. 3–21.

Miller, D. R., Swanson, G. E. (1958) *The Changing American Parent*, New York: John Wiley.

Riesman, D. (1950) *The Lonely Crowd*, New Haven, Conn.: Yale University Press; Oxford: OUP.

Strecker, E. A. (1946) *Their Mothers' Sons*, Philadelphia and Toronto: J. B. Lippincott.

2 Measuring intelligence

Anastasi, A. (1954) *Psychological Testing*, New York and London: Macmillan.

Bayley, N. (1949) 'Consistency and variability in the growth of intelligence from birth to eighteen years.' *J. gen. Psychol.*, **75**, pp. 165–96.

Berelson, B., Steiner, G. A. (1964) *Human Behaviour, An Inventory of Scientific Findings*, New York: Harcourt; Ontario: Longmans.

Cronbach, L. J. (1960) *Essentials of Psychological Testing*, 2nd edn. New York: Harper.

Goddard, H. H. (1912) *The Kallilak Family*, New York and London: Macmillan.

(1914) *Feeble-mindedness. Its Causes and Consequences*, New York and London: Macmillan.

Goodenough, F. L. (1949) *Mental Testing, Its History, Principles and Testing*, London: Staples Press; New York: Rinehart.

Hofstätter, P. R. (1954) 'The changing composition of intelligence.' *J. gen. Psychol.*, **85**, pp. 159–64.

Klineberg, O. (1951) *Race and Psychology. The Race Question in Modern Science*, Paris: UNESCO.

Meili, R. (1937) *Psychologische Diagnostik*, Munich: Reinhardt Verlag.

(1955) *Lehrbuch der Psychologischen Diagnostik*. 3rd edn. Bern: Huber.

Oléron, P. (1958) *Les Composantes de l'Intelligence d'après les Recherches Factorielles*, Paris: Presse Univers de France.

Spearman, C. (1927) *The Abilities of Man. Their Nature and Measurement*, New York and London: Macmillan.

244

Terman, L. M. (1916) *The Measurement of Intelligence*, Boston: Houghton Mifflin.

Terman, L. M., Merrill, M. A. (1937) *Measuring Intelligence*, Boston: Houghton Mifflin.

Thurstone, L. L. (1935) *The Vectors of Mind*, Chicago: University of Chicago Press.

(1947) *Multiple Factor Analysis*, Chicago: University of Chicago Press.

Vernon, P. E. (1950) *The Structure of Human Abilities*, London: Methuen; New York: John Wiley.

(1965) 'Ability and environment' *Amer. Psychol.*, **20**, pp. 723–33.

3 Defining intelligence

Bruner, J. S. (1964) 'The course of cognitive growth', *Amer. Psychol.* **19**, pp. 1–15.

Flavell, J. H. (1963) *The Developmental Psychology of Jean Piaget*, Princeton: Van Nostrand.

Goodnow, J. (1962) 'A test of milieu effects with some of Piaget's tasks', *Psychol. Monogr.*, **76**, pp. 1–22.

Inhelder, B. (1962) 'Some aspects of Piaget's genetic approach to cognition', *Monogr. Soc. Res. Child. Develop.*, **27** (2), pp. 19–40.

Janet, P. (1935) *Les Débuts de l'Intelligence*, Paris: Flammarion.

(1936) *L'Intelligence avant le Langage*, Paris: Flammarion.

Koffka, K. (1921) *Die Psychische Entwicklung des Kindes*, Osterwieck: Zickfeld.

McDougall, W. (1947) *An Outline of Psychology*, 11th edn., London: Methuen.

Meyerson, I. (1948) *Les Fonctions Psychologiques et les Oeuvres*, Paris: Vrin.

Piaget, J. (1950) *The Psychology of Intelligence*, London: Routledge and Kegan Paul; Paterson, N. J.: Littlefield, Adams (1960) (English translation of *La Psychologie de l'Intelligence*).

(1964) *Six Etudes de Psychologie*, Paris: Gonthier.

Smedlund, J. S. (1961) 'The acquisition of conservation of substance and weight in children' *Scand. J. Psychol.*, **2**, pp. 11–20, 71–87, 153–5, 156–60, 203–10.

Whorf, B. L. (1956) *Language, Thought and Reality*, Cambridge, Mass.: MIT Press.

4 The basic drives

Bronfenbrenner, U. (1960) 'Freudian theories of identification and their derivatives', *Child Develop.*, **31**, pp. 15–40.

Erikson, E. H. (n.d.) *Childhood and Society*, London: Imago Publications; New York: Norton (1950).

Heilbrun, A. B. (1965) 'The measurement of identification', *Child Develop.*, **36**, pp. 111–28.

Lawson, R. (1965) *Frustration, The Development of a Scientific Concept*, New York and London: Macmillan.

Mead, M. (1959) Sex and Temperament in Three Primitive Societies. London: Routledge and Kegan Paul; (1966) Gloucester, Mass: Peter Smith.

Mowrer, O. (1960) *Learning Theory and Behaviour*, New York: John Wiley; London: Chapman.

Parsons, T., Bales, R. F. (1955) *Family, Socialization and Interaction Process*, Glencoe: Free Press; Toronto: Burns & Mac Eachern.

Robert, M. (1966) *The Psychoanalytic Revolution: Sigmund Freud's Life and Achievement* (Translation of *La Révolution Psychoanalytique. La Vie et l'Oeuvre de Sigmund Freud*) London: Allen & Unwin.

Rosenzweig, S. (1945) 'The picture association method and its application in a study of reactions to frustration', *J. Personality*, **14**, pp. 3–23.

(1949) *Psychodiagnosis*, New York: Grune & Stratton.

Sewell, W. H., Mussen, P. H. (1952) 'The effect of feeding, weaning and scheduling procedures on childhood adjustment and the formation of oral symptoms', *Child Develop.*, **23**, pp. 185–91.

Whiting, J. W. M., Child, I. L. (1953) *Child Training and Personality*. New Haven, Conn.: Yale University Press; Toronto: Burns & Mac Eachern; Oxford: OUP.

5 Situations and relationships

Baldwin, A. L., Kalhorn, Y., Bresse, F. H. (1945) 'Patterns of parent behaviour', *Psychol. Monogr.*, **58**, (3).

(1949) 'Appraisal of parent behaviour', *Psychol. Monogr.*, **63**, (4).

Barker, R. G., Kounin, J. S., Wright, H. F. (1943) *Child Behaviour and Development*, New York: McGraw-Hill.

Barry, H., Child, I. L., Bacon, M. K. (1959) 'Relation of child training to subsistence economy', *Amer. Anthrop.*, **61**, pp. 51–63.

Becker, W. C. (1964) 'Consequences of different kinds of parental discipline', in Hoffman and Hoffman, see below.

Bossard, J. H. S. (1954) *The Sociology of Child Development*, 2nd edn. New York: Harper.

Bossard, J. H. S., Bolles, E. S. (1955) 'Personality roles in the large family', *Child Develop.*, **26**, pp. 71–8.

Caldwell, B. M. (1964) 'The effects of infant care', in Hoffman and Hoffman, see below.

Carmichael, L. (ed.) (1946) *Manual of Child Psychology*, New York: John Wiley; London: Chapman and Hall.

Hoffman, M. L., Hoffman, L. N. W. (1964) *Review of Child Development Research*, I, New York: Russell Sage Foundation.

Johnson, M. M. (1963) 'Sex role learning in the nuclear family', *Child Develop.*, **34**, pp. 319–33.

Kagan, J. (1964) 'American longitudinal research on psychological development', *Child Develop.*, **35**, pp. 1–32.

Koch, H. L. (1956) 'Children's work attitudes and siblings characteristics', *Child Develop.*, **27**, pp. 289–311.

(1956) 'Some emotional attitudes of the young child in relation to characteristics of his siblings', *Child Develop.*, **27,** pp. 393–427.

(1956) 'Sissiness and tomboyishness in relation to siblings characteristics', *J. genet. Psychol.*, **88,** pp. 231–45.

(1956) 'Attitudes of young children toward their peers as related to certain characteristics of their siblings', *Psychol. Monogr.*, **70**, p. 19.

Meili, R. (1957) *Die Anfänge der Charakterentwicklung*, Bern: Huber.

Miller, D. R., Swanson, G. E. (1958) *The Changing American Parent*, New York: John Wiley.

Murchison, C. (1931) (ed.) *A Handbook of Child Psychology*, Worcester: Clark University Press.

Nash, J. (1965) 'The father in contemporary culture and current psychological literature', *Child Develop.*, **36,** pp. 261–97.

Olson, W. C., Hughes, B. O. (1943) 'Growth of the child as a whole', in Barker, R. G., Kounin, J. S., Wright, H. F. (eds.) *Child Behaviour and Development*, New York: McGraw-Hill.

Osterrieth, P. A. (1964) *Faire des Adultes*, Brussels: Dessart.

Parsons, T., Bales, R. F. (1955) *Family, Socialization and Interaction Process*, Glencoe: Free Press; Toronto: Burns & Mac Eachern.

Roy, L. (1950) 'Parents' attitudes towards their children', *J. Home Econ.*, **42**, pp. 652–3.

Schaefer, E.S. (1965) 'A configurational analysis of childrens' reports of parent behaviour', *J.consult.Psychol.*, **29**, pp. 552–7.

Stevenson, H.W. (ed.) (1963) *Child Psychology*, Part I of 62nd Yearbook of the National Society for the Study of Education, Chicago: University of Chicago Press.

Stone, A.A., Onqué, G.C. (1959) *Longitudinal Studies of Child Personality*, Cambridge, Mass.: Harvard University Press; London: OUP.

6 What is normality?

Cole, L.E. (1953) *Human Behaviour*, Yonkers, N.Y.: World Books; London: Harrap.

Duykaerts, F. (1954) *La Notion de Normale en Psychologie Clinique*, Paris: Vrin.

Fromm, E. (1949) *Man for Himself*, London: Routledge and Kegan Paul; Toronto: Clarke, Irwin.

Gesell, A. (1943) *Infant and Child in the Culture of Today*, New York: Harper; London: Hamilton; Toronto: Mussen.

Gesell, A., Ilg, F.L. (1946) *The Child from Five to Ten*, 3rd edn. New York: Harper; London: Hamilton; Toronto: Mussen.

Gesell, A., Ilg, F.L., Ames, L.B. (1956) *Youth: the Years from 10 to 16*, New York: Harper; London: Hamilton.

Hebb, D.O. (1949) *The Organization of Behaviour*, New York: John Wiley; London: Chapman.

Hofstätter, P.R. (1965) *Sozialpsychologie*, Berlin: Goeschen and de Gruyter.

Mowrer, O. (1948) 'What is normal behaviour?' in Pennington, L.A., Berg, I.A. (eds.) *An Introduction to Clinical Psychology*, New York: Ronald Press.

Muller, P. (1963) *La Psychologie dans le Monde Moderne*, Brussels: Dessart.

Portmann, A. (1951) *Biologische Fragmente zu einer Lehre vom Menschen*. Basel: Schwabe. (Also revised edition (1956) retitled *Zoologie und das neue Bild des Menschen*. Rowohlts Deutsche Enzyklopaedie, No. 20.)

Saul, L.J. (1947) *Emotional Maturity*, Philadelphia: Lippincott.

7 The main divisions of childhood

Harlow, H.F. (1958) 'The nature of love', *Amer.Psychol.*, **13**, 673–85.

Havighurst, R.J. (1953) *Human Development and Education*, London and New York: Longmans, Green.

Kroh, O. (1928) *Die Psychologie des Grundschulkindes in ihrer Beziehung zur kindlichen Gesamtentwicklung*, Leipzig: Langen.

Minkowski, M. (1938) 'L'élaboration du système nerveux', in l'Encyclopédie Française, Vol. VIII, Sect. A., Chapter 1. Paris: Comité de l'Encyclopédie Française.

Mussen, P. H., Conger, J. J., Kagan, J. (1963) *Child Development and Personality*, 2nd edn. New York: Harper.

8 Infancy and its developmental tasks

Boutan, L. (1914) *Les Deux Méthodes de l'Enfant*, Bordeaux: Saugnac.

Braine, M. D. S. (1963) 'The ontogeny of English phrase structure', *Language*, **39**, pp. 1–13.

Brown, R. W. (1965) *Social Psychology*, New York: Free Press; New York and London: Macmillan.

Carmichael, L. (1951) 'Ontogenetive development', in Stevens, S. S. (ed.) *Handbook of Experimental Development*, New York: John Wiley, p. 281.

Chen, H., Irwin, O. (1946) 'Development of speech during infancy: curve of differential percentage indices', *J. exp. Psychol.*, **36**, pp. 522–5.

Claparede, E. (1905) *Psychologie de l'Enfant*, Geneva: Knudig. (Re-issued 1946–7 in two volumes by Delachaux & Niestlé: Neuchâtel.)

Dollard, J., Miller, N. E. (1905) *Personality and Psychotherapy*, New York: McGraw-Hill.

Dubin, E. R., Dubin, R. (1963) 'The authority inception period in socialization', *Child Develop.*, **34**, pp. 885–98.

Ervin, Miller. (1943) 'Language development', in chapter 3 of Stevenson, H. W. (ed.) *Child Psychology*, Chicago: University of Chicago Press.

Fantz, R. L. (1961) 'The origin of form perception', *Sci. Amer.*, **204**, pp. 66–72.

Geber, J. M. (1958) 'The psychomotor development of African children in the first year and the influence of maternal behaviour', *J. soc. Psychol.*, **47**, pp. 185–95.

Gesell, A. (1943) *Infant and Child in the Culture of Today*, New York: Harper; London: Hamilton; Toronto: Mussen.

Hebb, D. O. (1949) *The Organization of Behaviour*, New York: John Wiley; London: Chapman.

Irwin, O., Chen, H. (1947) 'Development of speech during infancy: curve of phonemic frequencies', *J.exp.Psychol.*, **37,** pp. 187–93.

Jacobson, R., Halle, M. (1956) *Fundamentals of Language*, 's Gravenhage: Mouton.

Leopold, W. F. (1939–49) *Speech Development of a Bilingual Child*, 4 Vols. Evanston, Ill.: Northwestern University.

Meili, R. (1957) *Die Anfänge der Charakterentwicklung*, Bern: Huber.

Richelle, M. (1966) *Le Conditionnement Opérant*, Neuchâtel: Delachaux and Niestlé.

Ruke-Dravina, V. (1963) *Zur Sprachentwicklung bei Kleinkindern*, Lund: Slaviska Institutionen vid Lund Universitet.

Sherman, M. (1927) 'The differentiation of emotional responses in infants', *J.comp.Psychol.*, **7,** pp. 265–84.

Velten, H. V. (1943) 'The growth of phonemic and lexical patterns in infant language', *Language*, **19,** pp. 281–92.

Whiting, J. W. M., Child, I. L. (1953) *Child Training and Personality*, New Haven, Conn.: Yale University Press; Toronto: Burns & Mac Eachern; London: OUP.

9 The school child and his developmental tasks

Allport, G. W. (1961) *Pattern and Growth in Personality*, New York: Holt, Rinehart & Winston.

Ames, L. B. (1952) 'The sense of self of nursery school children as manifested by their verbal behaviour', *J.gen.Psychol.*, **81,** pp. 193–232.

Ariès, P. (1960) *L'Enfant et la Vie Familiale sous l'Ancien Régime*, Paris: Plon.

Bühler, Ch. (1928) *Kindheit und Jugend*, Leipzig: Hirzel.

Chateau, J. (1946) *Le Réel et l'Imaginaire dans le Jeu de l'Enfant*, Paris: Vrin. (1947) *Le Jeu de l'Enfant après Trois Ans*, Paris: Vrin. (also 2nd edn., 1961).

Douglas, J. W. B., Ross, J. M. (1965) 'The effects of absence on primary school performance', *J.Educ.Psychol.*, **35,** pp. 28–40.

Dublineau, J. (1947) *Les Grandes Crises de l'Enfance*, Paris: Bloud and Gay.

English, H. B. (1962) *Dynamics of Child Development*, New York: Holt, Rinehart and Winston.

Fridan, B. (1963) *Feminine Mystique*, New York: Vision Press; French translation (1966) *La femme mystifiée*, Paris: Gonthier.

Gesell, A., Ilg, F. L. (1946) *The Child from Five to Ten*, 3rd edn., New York: Harper.

Hartshorne, H., May, M. A. (1928–30) *Character Education Enquiry*. Vol. 1. *Studies in Deceit*. Vol. 2. *Studies in Service and Self Control*. Vol. 3. *Studies in the Organisation of the Character*, New York and London: Macmillan.

Jones, M. C. (1960) 'A comparison of the attitudes and interests of ninth grade students over two decades', *J. Educ. Psychol.*, **51**, pp. 175–86.

Kinsey, A. C., Pomeroy, J. W. B., Martin, C. E. (1948) *Sexual Behaviour in the Human Male*, Philadelphia: W. B. Saunders.

Muller, P. (1958) *Le CAT. – Recherches sur le Dynamisme Enfantin*, Bern: Huber.

Newcomb, T. M. (1929) 'The consistency of certain extrovert-introvert behaviour patterns in 53 problem boys', *Teach. Coll. Contrib. Educ.*, No. 282.

Piaget, J. (1932) *Le Jugement Moral chez l'Enfant*, Paris; F. Alcan.
The Moral Judgment of The Child, London: Routledge and Kegan Paul

Rousson, M. (1966) *Milieux Sociaux et Compétences*, Neuchâtel: Messeiller.

Sanderson, A. E. (1963) 'The idea of reading readiness: a re-examination', *Educ. Res.*, **6**, pp. 3–9.

Schelsky, H. (1955) *Soziologie der Sexualität*, Hamburg: Rowohlt.

Scupin, E., Scupin, G. (1907 *Bubi's Erste Kindheit*, Leipzig: Th. Grieben.
(1910) *Bubi im 4 nach 6 Lebensjahre*, Leipzig: Th. Greben.

Templin, M. C. (1957) *Certain Language Skills in Children – Their Development and Inter-Relationships*, Institute of Child Welfare Monograph Series, No. 26. Minneapolis: University of Minnesota.

Thackeray, D. V. (1965) 'The relationship between reading readiness and reading progress', *Brit. J. Educ. Psychol.*, **35**, pp. 232–4.

Wallon, H. (1925) *L'Enfant Turbulent*, Paris: F. Alcan.

10 Adolescence

Arendt, H. (1960) *Vita Activa oder vom Tätigen Leben*. Stuttgart: Kohlhammer.

Chesterton, G. K. (1910) *What's Wrong with the World*, London and New York: Cassell.

Debesse, M. (1936) *La Crise d'Originalité Juvénile*, Paris: F. Alcan.
(1942) *L'Adolescence*, Paris; Presse Univers de France.

Erikson, E. H. (n.d.) *Childhood and Society*, London: Imago Publications; New York: Norton (1950).

Gesell, A., Ilg, F. L., Ames, L. B. (1956) *Youth: The Years from 10 to 16*, New York: Harper; London: Hamish Hamilton.

Hollingshead, A. B. (1949) *Elmtown's Youth*, New York: John Wiley; London: Chapman.

Klages, L. (1929–32) *Der Geist als Widersacher der Seele*, Leipzig: Barth.

Lessing, Th. (1930) *Europa und Asia, Untergang der Erde am Geist*, Leipzig: Meiner.

Muchow, H. H. (1959) *Sexualreife und Sozialstruktur der Jugend*, Rowohlts Deutsche Enzyklopaedie, No. 94. Hamburg: Rowohlt.

(1962) *Jugend und Zeitgeist*, Rowohlts Deutsche Enzyklopaedie, No. 147/8, Hamburg: Rowohlt.

Muller, P. (1956) *Itinéraire Philosophique*, Neuchâtel: La Bacconière.

Murray, H. A. (1938) *Explorations in Personality*, London OUP.

Parsons, T., Bales, R. F. (1955) *Family Socialization and Interaction Process*, Glencoe: Free Press; Toronto: Burns and Mac Eachern.

Runner, J. R. (1937) 'Social distance in adolescent relationships', *Amer. J. Social.*, **43**, pp. 418–39.

Scheler, M. (1929) *Philosophische Weltanschauung*. Bonn: Cohen.

Acknowledgments

Acknowledgment is due to the following sources for diagrams which have been copied or adopted in this book (numbers are figure-numbers): 1 F. Baade *La Course à l'an 2000*, Presse Universale de France; 2,6 *Encyclopédie française permanente*; 9 Roland Pressat *L'analyse démographique*, *PUF*; 11,49,50,51,60 Mussen, Conger and Kagan *Child Development and Personality*, Harper & Row; 12,13 J. Bayley 'Consistency and variability in the growth of intelligence', *Journal of General Psychology*; 15 *Guide to the Use of the GATB*, US Department of Labor; 16 P. R. Hofstaetter 'The changing composition of intelligence', *JGP*; 17,34,37,40,52,53,54 G. G. Thompson *Child Development*, Houghton Mifflin; 21,22 J. Bruner 'The course of cognitive growth', *American Psychologist*; 25,26,27,28 E. H. Erikson *Childhood and Society*, Imago Publications; 30,31 F. V. Smith *The Explanation of Human Behaviour*, Constable; 32 Barker, Dembo and Lewin, in Barker, Kounin and Wright *Child Behaviour and Development*, McGraw-Hill; 36 Parsons and Bales *Family*, Free Press; 38,39 Hoffman and Hoffman *Review of child development research*, vol. 1 (chapter by Becker), Russell Sage Foundation and *Journal of Abnormal and Social Psychology*; 42 Carmichael *Manual of Child Psychology*, John Wiley; 47 *Scientific American*; 48 Dubin and Dubin 'The authority inception period in socialisation', *Child Development*; 55 R. Brown *Social Psychology*, Free Press; 56,57 Miller *Language and Communication*, McGraw-Hill; 70 Cole *Psychology of Adolescence*, Reinhard; 73,74 P. Muller, BASC. The diagrams were prepared by Design Practitioners Limited.

Acknowledgment for photographs – further to any made in the captions – is also due to: frontispiece, 62 Derek Bayes/Observer; 7,15,23 Mansell Collection; 8 UNICEF, New York; 10 Larousse; 19 Revue Suisse de Psychologie; 29,45 Camera Press; 33 Exposition Press Inc; 41 Fox Photos; 43 *American Psychologist*; 44 William Heinemann Ltd; 46 David Linton and *Scientific American*; 58,59,63,64,66,68,71,72 Andrew Lanyon; 61 Jane Bown/Observer; 67,69 (left) Barnaby's Picture Library.

Index

Books published or in preparation

Economics and Social Studies

The World Cities
Peter Hall, *London*

The Economics of Underdeveloped Countries
Jagdish Bhagwati, *MIT*

Development Planning
Jan Tinbergen, *Rotterdam*

Human Communication
J. L. Aranguren, *Madrid*

Education in the Modern World
John Vaizey, *London*

Money
Roger Opie, *Oxford*

Soviet Economics
Michael Kaser, *Oxford*

Decisive Forces in World Economics
J. L. Sampedro, *Madrid*

Key Issues in Criminology
Roger Hood, *Durham*

Population and History
E. A. Wrigley, *Cambridge*

History

The Emergence of Greek Democracy
W. G. Forrest, *Oxford*

Muhammad and the Conquests of Islam
Francesco Gabrieli, *Rome*

The Civilisation of Charlemagne
Jacques Boussard, *Poitiers*

The Crusades
Geo Widengren, *Uppsala*

The Ottoman Empire
Halil Inalcik, *Ankara*

Humanism in the Renaissance
S. Dresden, *Leyden*

The Rise of Toleration
Henry Kamen, *Warwick*

The Scientific Revolution 1500-1700
Hugh Kearney, *Sussex*

The Left in Europe
David Caute, *London*

The Rise of the Working Class
Jürgen Kuczynski, *Berlin*

Chinese Communism
Robert North, *Stanford*

The Italian City Republics
Daniel Waley, *London*

The Culture of Japan
Mifune Okumura, *Kyoto*

The History of Persia
Jean Aubin, *Paris*

The Dutch Republic
Charles Wilson, *Cambridge*

The Arts

The Language of Modern Art
Ulf Linde, *Stockholm*

Twentieth Century Music
H. H. Stuckenschmidt, *Berlin*

Art Nouveau
S. Tschudi Madsen, *Oslo*

Palaeolithic Cave Art
P. J. Ucko and A. Rosenfeld, *London*

Primitive Art
Eike Haberland, *Mainz*

Expressionism
John Willett, *London*

Language and Literature

French Literature
Raymond Picard, *Paris*

**Russian Writers and Society
1825–1904**
Ronald Hingley, *Oxford*

Satire
Matthew Hodgart, *Sussex*

The Romantic Century
Robert Baldick, *Oxford*

Philosophy and Religion

Christian Monasticism
David Knowles, *London*

Witchcraft
Lucy Mair, *London*

Sects
Bryan Wilson, *Oxford*

Earth Sciences and Astronomy

The Structure of the Universe
E. L. Schatzman, *Paris*

Climate and Weather
H. Flohn, *Bonn*

Anatomy of the Earth
André Cailleux, *Paris*

Zoology and Botany

Mimicry in plants and animals
Wolfgang Wickler. *Seewiesen*

Lower Animals
Martin Wells, *Cambridge*

The World of an Insect
Rémy Chauvin, *Strasbourg*

Primates
François Bourlière, *Paris*

The Age of the Dinosaurs
Björn Kurtén, *Helsinki*

Psychology and Human Biology

Eye and Brain
R. L. Gregory, *Edinburgh*

The Ear and the Brain
E. C. Carterette, *UCLA*

The Biology of Work
O. G. Edholm, *London*

The Psychology of Fear and Stress
J. A. Gray, *Oxford*

Doctor and Patient
P. Lain Entralgo, *Madrid*

Chinese Medicine
P. Huard and M. Wong, *Paris*

Physical Science and Mathematics

Particles and Accelerators
Robert Gouiran, *CERN, Geneva*

The Quest for Absolute Zero
K. Mendelssohn, *Oxford*

What is Light ?
A. C. S. van Heel and
C. H. F. Velzel, *Eindhoven*

Mathematics Observed
Hans Freudenthal, *Utrecht*

Waves and Corpuscles
J. L. Andrade e Silva and G. Lochak,
Paris   Introduction by Louis de Broglie

Applied Science

Words and Waves
A. H. W. Beck, *Cambridge*

The Science of Decision-making
A. Kaufmann, *Paris*

Bionics
Lucien Gérardin, *Paris*

Data Study
J. L. Jolley, *London*

Metals and Civilisation
R. W. Cahn, *Sussex*